Screenplay Library

Edited by Matthew J. Bruccoli
Irwin R. Blacker, Consulting Editor

F. Scott Fitzgerald's

Screenplay for

Three
Comrades

By

Erich Maria Remarque

Edited, with an Afterword by
Matthew J. Bruccoli

SOUTHERN ILLINOIS UNIVERSITY PRESS
Carbondale and Edwardsville
Feffer & Simon, Inc., London and Amsterdam

791.437
F55t

Library of Congress Cataloging in Publication Data

Fitzgerald, Francis Scott Key, 1896-1940.
  F. Scott Fitzgerald's screenplay for Three comrades.

  (Screenplay library)
  "Fitzgerald's movie work": p.
  I. Bruccoli, Matthew Joseph, 1931-
II. Remarque, Erich Maria, 1869-1970. Drei Komraden. III. Three comrades.
[Motion picture] IV. Title. V. Title: Three Comrades. VI. Series.
PN1997.T47   1978   813'.5'2   77-28077
ISBN 0-8093-0854-1
ISBN 0-8093-0853-3 pbk.

Designed by Gary Gore

MB

Contents

ACKNOWLEDGMENTS

The editor acknowledges the generous
assistance of Jeremy Nussbaum of
Greenbaum, Wolff & Ernst, Roger Mayer of
Metro-Goldwyn-Mayer, Herbert S. Nussbaum
of Metro-Goldwyn-Mayer, Paulette Goddard
Remarque, R. L. Samsell, Jeanne Bennett, and
Fletcher Markle. Mrs. Ben Hamilton of
Hampton Books provided the illustrations for
this volume.

Preface

By Irwin R. Blacker

There is in the F. Scott Fitzgerald correspondence about *Three Comrades* an incredible innocence, as well as the integrity of an artist working in a field where he has not the final say over his work. Fitzgerald must have known by the time he went to work on *Three Comrades* that what the studio—as represented by producer Joseph Mankiewicz—wanted was not quality or believable characters, but a picture that would satisfy the desires of a mass audience. Fitzgerald was hired to adapt a novel into a screenplay, and Mankiewicz was responsible for making a film that would bring in an audience.

The writer who becomes so emotionally involved in his screenplay may be honest, sincere, and have other artistic virtues; but, as with Fitzgerald, those are not the ones sought by the studios. His deep concern about his dialogue being true to the characters indicates a lack of understanding on several levels. The unity of his characters would not have meant as much to viewers as Fitzgerald believed; and a novelist's dialogue is rarely used in film, as the very nature of dramatic dialogue is different from the novelist's and serves a different purpose.

The version of *Three Comrades* published here is not a screenplay in the sense that it is not a finished blueprint for the making of a motion picture. The motion picture was eventually filmed from the shooting script that evolved from the collaboration of Fitzgerald, and E. E. Paramore—with Mankiewicz' final revisions. It has been customary in the film industry to use the talents of novelists to assist in adaptations or even write original stories for film. These served as the basis of the work eventually completed by professional screenwriters, in many instances wonderful craftsmen. (Mankiewicz went on to win Academy Awards in consecutive years for *All About Eve* and *Letter to Three Wives*.)

The *Three Comrades* script has value for the study of adaptation. Whereas the novelist need not limit the number of crises which make up his tale, the screenwriter generally must hold to about twenty-five, averaging about five pages a scene. This requirement means that Fitzgerald had to restructure the Remarque novel into a dramatic form with all of the requirements of the motion picture script: conflict, opening exposition, rise to a climax, character change, and denouement. In addition, he had to make visual what the novelist had the liberty of placing in a character's head. Fitzgerald was not deeply concerned with the proper script form. In all probability, he was not even expected to create a shooting script, as M.G.M. knew that his version would be reworked by someone else who better understood the problems of production.

In recent years the script has been simplified, so that the technical knowledge which was once expected of the writer is no longer important. The screenwriters write in master scenes, not bothering to call for new camera shots when everything takes place in one location. The writer knows the scene will be shot several times from several different directions, and there is no way he can describe that or hold a director to a visual concept. Also, the contemporary script increasingly leaves out all camera directions, as the writer has become more concerned with what is taking place on the screen than with how it gets there. For that reason, this F. Scott Fitzgerald script is interesting for its historical value, as well as its insights into how one novelist reworked the structure of another novelist into a dramatic form. If the reader has the interest to look at the work with care, he will place the novel and the screenplay side by side and compare the changes to see how the adaptation was accomplished. At no time should the reader of this screenplay forget that what he is reading was never intended to be a work of literature, but the sketch for a blueprint—which other writers turned into the final blueprint from which the director and film crew created a motion picture.

EDITORIAL NOTE

The copy-text for this edition of the *Three Comrades* screenplay is the Metro-Goldwyn-Mayer mimeographed typescript dated 9/1/37. Spelling, punctuation, and obvious typing errors have been silently emended; the German words required special attention. Eight substantive emendations have been made:

    4:8 cue [queue

    16:21 fifteen [sixteen

    41:14 lease [last

    116:20 Otto [Gottfried

    141:17 of [an

    186:26 hold [holds

    187:28 Now now. [Not now.

    213:26 sat [set

    233:17 Buon Mattina [Buon giorno

The novel umlauts *Köster,* but the name is given as *Koster* throughout Fitzgerald's screenplay.

Metro-Goldwyn-Mayer Inc.

Three Comrades

From:

F. Scott Fitzgerald

9/1/37

C A S T

Erich Lohkamp	Robert Taylor
Patricia Hollmann	Margaret Sullavan
Otto Koster	Franchot Tone
Gottfried Lenz	Robert Young
Dr. Becker	Henry Hull
Aftons	Guy Kibbee
Breuer	Lionel Atwill
Mrs. Schultz	Sarah Padden
Local Doctor	Charley Grapewin
Dr. Jaffé	Monty Woolley

Three Comrades

1   FADE IN:
     A GERMAN FLAG —

     — surmounted by a MAGNIFICENT BRONZE IM-
     PERIAL EAGLE, waving against a white sky.
                                        CUT TO:

2   A FRENCH SEVENTY-FIVE GUN —

     — in action. It fires.
                                        CUT TO:

3   THE FLAGPOLE —

     — newly split, the eagle gone, the shredded flag
     fluttering on the remnant of the pole.
                                    DISSOLVE TO:

4   A CORNER OF A MILITARY WAREHOUSE —

     — where a pile of rifles mounts rapidly higher as
     other rifles are laid upon it.
                                        CUT TO:

5   A PILE OF GERMAN HELMETS —

     — added to as other helmets are thrown upon it.
                                    DISSOLVE TO:

6 TITLE:
"DURING THE NINETEEN-TWENTIES WHILE
THE WORLD WAS PROSPEROUS THE GER-
MANS WERE A BEATEN AND IMPOVER-
ISHED PEOPLE."

DISSOLVE TO:

7 EXT. OF A FOOD DEPOT; THE BEGINNING OF
AN ENDLESS QUEUE OF PEOPLE —

— the poor, the middle-class, returned soldiers,
children, tramps, all waiting with baskets or ret-
icules in a quarter-mile bread-line. It turns a corner
and winds around a block as the CAMERA
TRUCKS along beside it.

At the very end are a rather haughty aristocratic
woman and a lovely, thin, wan-faced little girl of
about thirteen who looks on the verge of starvation.
A Red Cross Doctor struck by the distinguished
aspect of the unhappy pair, stops for a moment
beside them.

Doctor

That little girl needs white bread and potatoes.
A demobilized officer and two soldiers overhear
the conversation as they pass along the sidewalk
and pause.

The Woman (with a short, scornful laugh)

What, bread! — Is there such a thing? And potatoes — this
child wouldn't recognize a potato if she saw one.

The Doctor (very sadly)

Ach! Later in life these growing children will suffer for all
this.

CUT TO:

8 THE THREE SOLDIERS —

— saddened. The officer, most matured of the three, wears a head bandage. His name is Otto Koster. The second, impetuous, fiery and smouldering, decorated with the Iron Cross of both classes, is Gottfried Lenz. The youngest, still lighthearted and carefree after a short experience at the front, is Bobby* Lohkamp. We only establish the three as a group and immediately —

DISSOLVE TO:

9 A GRAPH —

— to show the passage of ten years. A line drawn from the upper left to the lower right of the graph, is marked "National Wealth of Germany." A moving pen draws another line which crosses the first line and moves always upward. This line is marked "Cost of Living." As this insert is primarily for a time lapse, the dates on the graph should be very large. When the pen stops under *1928* —

DISSOLVE TO:

10 A SIGN READING: "GASOLINE, 1 M. 40 Pfg."

We hear a full-bellied laugh of derision. The CAMERA PANS DOWN to show an automobile in front of a suburban filling station. It is a paintless touring car with split fenders that do not match, and windshield patched with adhesive tape.

In it sit the Three Comrades, wearing mechanics' jumpers. They are a little older. Koster wears eyeglasses and shows a large scar on his forehead.

* Bobby's name was changed to Erich in the later revises.—Ed.

Bobby Lohkamp is the sprucer of the three, even to sporting a flower behind his ear. The man laughing is the filling station attendant, holding a water-can. The Comrades look at him with an expression which says, "Funny, are we? Oh yeah?"

The Attendant (convulsed)

That ain't one car. That's made out of ten cars. You ought to have ten licenses. Should I give you a push?

Pityingly the Comrades exchange a glance. Then Otto Koster steps on it, Bobby Lohkamp flicks the flower at the attendant, and they leave the filling station in such a burst of speed that the man jumps back and stares in astonishment.

CUT TO:

11　　A SUBURBAN ROAD. AFTERNOON

The Comrades, bowling along leisurely, are passed by a reckless motor-cyclist, veering from one side of the road to the other. He holds his place annoyingly in front of the Comrades' car, which will shortly be introduced as "Heinrich";* and the Comrades don't like it. We come to:

12　　A CROSSROAD ON A RISE OF GROUND.

Neither city nor country; a few scattered houses and signboards.

The car, "Heinrich," approaches. It begins to pass the cyclist, but slows up at the crossroad warning. But the motorcyclist curves narrowly around in front of a Ford coming out of the side road, and goes on his way.

* *Note:* I have put "Heinrich" instead of "Karl" because the latter is so like "car" that it would be a source of confusion.

CUT TO:

13 A CLOSE UP OF THE COMRADES IN THEIR CAR.

Koster

Look at that half-wit!

Lenz

That's done it!

CUT TO:

14 THE FORD FROM THE SIDE ROAD —

— skids and overturns smashingly in the road.

CUT TO:

15 KOSTER —

— slams on his brakes and barely avoids crashing into the overturned car. Instantly the three Comrades jump out and run to the wreck. Koster has a slight limp.

CUT TO:

THE DRIVER OF THE FORD —

— Puppi, a baker about fifty, soft, stout, sharp-looking, unattractive, is pinned between the wheel and the seat. The motor is still running at high speed, but as Lenz turns it off, the man's groans are audible. Koster, an exceptionally strong man, bends back the wheel while the other two pull Puppi out.

Lenz

Easy now.

Bobby Lohkamp (gritting his teeth)

His ribs are crushed — I can feel.

Koster (panting)

There's a hospital up the road.
          They place the man in "Heinrich".

Koster (to Bobby)

You stay here and keep an eye on it.
          (he indicates the wreck)
May mean a repair job for us.
          Koster drives off, with Lenz beside him, holding
          the half-unconscious baker in his arms.
                               DISSOLVE TO:

17   INT. THE RECEPTION ROOM OF A SMALL
          HOSPITAL.

          The injured man is on an examination table. The
          Doctor looks up and speaks to Koster and Lenz.

The Doctor

Might have been worse. Couple of ribs broken. He'd better
stay here.

Puppi (feebly)

What about my car?
          (to Lenz and Koster)
Will you see about the car?
          (struggles for breath)
Telephone a garage.

Lenz (hinting)

We run a repair shop ourselves.

Koster

We'll tow it in if you want us to take care of it for you.

Puppi

All right — all right. Do what's necessary. My name's Manfred Puppi.

Koster (taking out a card)

My name's Otto Koster.
         (puts the card in Puppi's pocket)

Lenz (consolingly)

It was the motorcycle's fault, and we've got his number.
                                    DISSOLVE TO:

18   THE ROAD. KOSTER AND LENZ —

        — driving rapidly back to the damaged car.

Koster

This is a God-send. First job in a week. I don't mind saying I've been uneasy.

Lenz

So have I — you lose your nerve on one meal a day.

Koster

And it's a big job too — radiator smashed, wheel crushed —
        (he breaks off)

What's the excitement?

   Lenz, staring ahead, sees:

19   THE SUBURBAN CROSSROADS

   People have gathered around the wrecked car.
   Bobby, his arms folded, stands defiantly in front
   of it. Facing him are four men in mechanics'
   clothes, tough eggs with mean fighting faces. A
   wrecking truck, marked "Vogt Brothers" is drawn
   up behind them.

The Biggest Vogt Brother (to Bobby)

Get going, or we'll push your face in!

Bobby

I told you this was our job.

            CUT TO:

20   "Heinrich" —

   — coming to rest beside the group.

Koster (to Lenz)

Looks like a tough bunch. They're going to need persuasion.
Where's a wrench?

   He takes off his glasses and groping for a wrench,
   puts it in his rear pocket.

Lenz (indignant)

The dirty robbers!

    (he closes his hand on a bunch of keys)
Too bad I've got on my best shoes.

Koster (getting out)

Watch it — we're three against four.

21   KOSTER AND LENZ —

— approaching the wreck.

Biggest Vogt (to Bobby)

Don't talk tripe or you'll need repairs yourself.
       Koster and Lenz range themselves beside Bobby.

Koster

We've got permission from the owner to do the job.

Another Vogt Brother (producing a tire wrench from behind his back)

How would you like another scar on your fat face?

Koster

That took a machine gun.

Biggest Vogt (still sure of himself)

Three of you, eh?

Lenz

No, four.

Another Brother (looking around)

Go on — he's kidding.

Lenz (dryly)

You can't see him — his name is Justice.

Biggest Vogt (to his brother)

Give us that trolley.

> One brother takes hold of the cable that swings
> from his derrick and walks forward. Bobby stands
> in his way — Vogt tries to shove by, and in a minute,
> the fight is on. It is a great fight — three canny
> veterans against four young toughs. We get flashes
> of:

22   KOSTER —

> — fighting coolly on two fronts, starting to use his
> wrench and deciding not to.

23   BOBBY —

> — down, apparently being choked to death, then
> free, and up again.

24   LENZ —

      — attacked with a tire wrench, knocking the man
      out with his improvised brass knuckles.

25   ONE OF THE BYSTANDERS —

      — a goofy, goggle-eyed peasant, jumping up and
      down and clapping in ecstacy whenever the battle
      turns in favor of the Comrades, almost weeping
      when it goes against them.

26   THE FIGHT —

      — has moved forward from the wrecked car toward
      the Vogt brothers' truck, which is parked on an
      incline. One Vogt is out cold. When Koster is
      momentarily free, he glances at Lenz who is fight-
      ing near the rear of the truck and has his opponent
      at a disadvantage.

Koster (crooks his finger and shouts to Lenz)

The crane!

      Lenz, struggling with his opponent, sees that
      the hook of the derrick hangs free on its cable.
      He suddenly understands and, reaching for the
      hook, attaches it to the man's belt.

27   SIMULTANEOUSLY:
      KOSTER —

      — has unset the emergency brake of the wrecking
      truck and given it a shove. The truck starts to roll
      and the Vogt brother gives a yell as he is pulled
      off with it, bumping along the ground.

28   THE OTHER BROTHERS —

— see, and yelling imprecations, start after their truck. As it passes out of the picture down the hill with one of them climbing aboard —

CUT TO:

29   THE THREE COMRADES —

— laughing in victory while the goofy peasant jumps up and down, clapping his hands with delight.

Koster

Now we'll take the prize to port.

DISSOLVE TO:

30   EXT. KOSTER & CO. AUTO REPAIR SHOP

The shop is set in a factory district of tall chimneys
and tenements. In front of it is the sign, and a
gas pump is in front of an old, creaking gate. As
Koster drives "Heinrich" in, pulling the wrecked
Ford, we follow to:

31   THE REPAIR SHOP
      A COURTYARD —

— in a canyon between big buildings. Part of it
is a covered shed sheltering a couple of dismantled
jallopies and a once-expensive Cadillac which pre-
serves a certain gaudy style and is polished to a
fare-you-well. It bears a sign, "For Sale." In a
corner is a one-story room which serves as an
office. Under a tin roof extending from it are chairs
and a rough table. Nearby, a sink with mechanics'
soap. As the caravan halts, we see:

32   MATILDA —

— the charwoman, swaying rather drunkenly in the
door of the office, then precipitately retiring.

Jupp, a boy of fifteen, freckled and spinakereared,
coming forward eagerly as he wipes his hands on
a piece of waste.

Jupp (before they can get out)

A customer! — A customer! A guy came to look at the Cad-
illac!
              (he points toward it)
He'll be back.
              (he stares at the Ford)
Whew!

Koster (getting out of "Heinrich")

We picked it up on the road. It means pay for you, Jupp.
          Jupp looks at their dishevelled clothes, then at the
          car and at Bobby, who has a bruised cheek bone.

Jupp

Were you *in* the wreck?

Bobby

We were in a war. And we need a drink.
                    (as he starts toward the sink)
Fine business on my birthday.

Lenz (calling after him)

Your birthday? How old?

Bobby (turning)

Thirty.

Lenz

How do you feel?

Bobby (washing his hands at the sink)

I feel like sixty and sixteen at once. I feel low as that creeper.
                    (he kicks at a roller, used to get under cars)

Lenz (calling)

What do you mean, low? If you're sixteen and sixty both,
you're living two lives at once.
                    (pause)
It's a miracle.
                    (Bobby disappears into the office)

Koster

Let him alone, Gottfried. Birthdays are no fun. That's when you look at yourself in the mirror and find you're only the same old heel after all. Let's get busy.
>   (to Jupp)
What's this about a customer?

Jupp

He said he'd be right back.

Lenz

Great snakes! If we can sell it, we can even pay the rent. Never mind the wreck. One more polish and we can ask another hundred.

Koster

Thick oil in the engine.

Lenz

More grease in the gears.

Koster

Deflate the tires for rough roads.

Lenz

Oil the bonnet. Hot water in the radiator.
>   They look toward the Cadillac with growing ex-
>   citement as they talk.

Koster

Come on, Gottfried!
>   He and Lenz spring for the work shed.

CUT TO:

33   THE DINGY BUT SUNLIT OFFICE

A desk, surmounted by silver framed photograph of the Comrades in uniform; some chairs; street clothes on hooks and hangers; an open cupboard and a small table on which rests an empty bottle. We hear a woman's voice, singing "The Song of the Bold Hussar," which dies hollowly away as the SCENE WIDENS to include Bobby coming in the door and Matilda, the charwoman, with her hand stretched toward the bottle. Seeing him, she stops, teetering like a drunken hippopotamus, and drops a broom from her other hand. She wears a dirty white headcloth, hitched-up skirt, apron and thick slippers.

Bobby (amused and annoyed)

Why, Frau Stoes! Last night that bottle was full. I must have forgotten to lock it up.

Matilda (blinking and staring)

Holy Saints! I wasn't expecting you.

Bobby

Evidently not. Was it good?

Matilda (involuntarily)

It sure was.
>   (recovering her dignity and wiping her
>   mouth)
This is very embarrassing. I simply can't understand it —

Bobby

I can. You're tight as a tick.

Matilda (at last thinking what to say)

I only smelled it at first, Herr Lohkamp. Then I took a nip for my sciatica. Then the Devil got hold of me.
                    (she draws herself up)
Anyhow, you ought not to lead an old woman into temptation, leaving bottles about.

Bobby

It isn't the first time.
                    (he takes another bottle from the cupboard
                    and looks at it)
You drank Herr Koster's best — and left the stuff we give to customers.

Matilda (grinning)

I know what's good. But you won't tell, will you, Herr Lohkamp? — and me a poor widow?

Bobby

Not this time.
            Jupp bursts into the office.

Jupp

Herr Lohkamp! The customer — the customer!
            He is closely followed by Lenz and Koster.

Lenz (to Bobby)

We've got to sell that Cadillac.
                    (his eyes, shining with an idea, rove around
                    the office)

CUT TO:

34   THE GATE —

— through which Blumenthal has just entered, looking about with the canny eye of a successful middle-aged business man. He has a dead-pan but not without humor.

35   THE OFFICE

Koster brushing his hair. Bobby looking out the window into the court.

Bobby

Look at that expression. Suspicious already.

Lenz (out of sight)

Remember the prices. Ask seven thousand. If he's a low cur, take forty-five hundred; if he's a maniac, forty-four hundred. But at that price, a curse goes with it. Go down fighting with your fist on his wallet.

Koster

Right.
                    (he goes out)

Lenz (still out of sight)

I'm going to put on an act.
                    Bobby follows Koster out.

CUT TO:

36   KOSTER —

— coming out of the office into the courtyard and meeting Blumenthal.

Koster (cordially)

My name's Koster.

Blumenthal (offering his hand)

Blumenthal.

Koster

You've come about the Cadillac?
                    (Blumenthal nods)
She's over here.

Blumenthal (dryly)

So I see.
          Koster gives him an appraising glance. They have
          walked across the courtyard. Bobby has started the
          engine of the car.

Koster (taking a long breath)

Good motor, good tires, good paint, dandy running condition.
And for a big body, that hood is remarkably light.
                    (he turns off the engine and raises the hood)
See, you can work it with one hand.
                    (but he and Bobby struggle with four hands
                    to close it. Then Koster bangs the doors
                    and rattles the handles)
Nothing worn. Tight as a glove. Try them.
                    (he takes his hand away. The handle comes
                    with it. He hastily replaces it. Bobby turns
                    on the engine again. Blumenthal nods in
                    a bored way)
Windows stay put at any height. Unbreakable glass — and
that's something —
                    (he points at the battered Ford)
— Why only today on the road —

Blumenthal (uninterested)

All cars have unbreakable glass.

Koster (a little nervously)

Horn —
                    (Bobby sounds it)
— pockets, seats, switchboard, lighter — Have a cigarette?

Blumenthal

I don't smoke.

                                        CUT TO:

37   THE GATE

            — which Lenz is banging shut as if he had just
            come in. He has removed his unionalls and is
            amazingly spruced up — coat, tie, hat, cane and
            pigskin gloves. He compares the office number
            with a newspaper in his hand and walks up to
            Koster.

Lenz

Is there a Cadillac for sale here?
                    (Koster nods, speechless)
Can I see it?

Bobby (playing up)

Here it is. But perhaps you won't mind waiting a minute.
Have a seat in the office.
            Lenz listens to the engine which is still humming.
            His face is critical, then appreciative. He nods and
            goes toward the office.

Blumenthal (practically)

What's the car cost?

Koster

Seven thousand marks —
              (more sternly)
Seven thousand marks net.

Blumenthal (snorting)

Too much.

Koster

If you drove it, you'd feel differently. How about a trial run?

Blumenthal

Trial runs don't prove anything. After you buy it you find out what's the matter.
              (Bobby and Koster look dismayed)
No, I'll call you up. Good morning.
              To their distress he suddenly turns away and strides very quickly out of the courtyard.

Koster (starting after him too late)

Now, Mr. Blumenthal —
              Mr. Blumenthal passes through the gate.
                                        CUT TO:

38   THE OFFICE DOOR

              Lenz coming out. He is hatless and coatless and is getting back into his work suit. The cane still dangles from his arm.

Lenz (proud of himself)

Well? How did I do? I saw you were up against it, and I thought I'd lend a hand.

Koster (glum at missing the sale)

I recognized my new suit.

Bobby

Where did you get the hot gloves?

Lenz

The Tax Collector left them. The cane too —
          (he brandishes it; then breaks off suddenly
          and stares toward the gate)

Bobby (oblivious to this)

You ought to go into vaudeville.
          He sees the look in Lenz's eye and turns; Blu-
          menthal has come back in and is striding briskly
          across the court.

Koster (nervously)

Oh — hello, Mr. Blumenthal.

Blumenthal (glancing at Lenz with amusement)

I see — you make your customers work for you. All joking aside, what do you want for that bus?

Bobby (sternly)

Seven thousand marks.

Koster (less sternly)

Six thousand marks.

Blumenthal

I'll give you five thousand.
> The Comrades groan.

Koster (pleadingly)

Five thousand eight hundred.

Blumenthal

Five thousand five hundred — and you're tickled to death.
I could easily knock you down another thousand.
> (a pause — the Comrades look at each other.
> They agree in silence)

It's a go! I want it in three days — license, new plates and
all.

Koster (really pleased)

Sold! And we'll throw in these cut-glass ash trays.
> (he takes one from a shelf and holds it up)
>> DISSOLVE TO:

A GLASS OF FOAMING BEER —

> — held aloft by Koster. The Comrades and Jupp,
> with Matilda in the background, are gathered
> around the outdoor table.

Koster

— So I am proud to say that on the occasion of his thirtieth
birthday, Bobby Lohkamp becomes a full-fledged member of
the firm of Koster and Company.
> (cheers)

Lenz (indicating bottles on the table)

This stuff is as old as he is — and too good for this lousy

hole. I move we go and have supper in the country — finish up a big day in the great outdoors. If we each take two bottles and put them in Heinrich, the road-spook —

General approval, as we

DISSOLVE TO:

40   "HEINRICH," THE AUTOMOBILE —

— rolling leisurely along a country road at twilight. The Comrades are in street clothes. Koster is driving; Lenz is looking at a newspaper and singing with Bobby.

Lenz and Bobby (in chorus)

Hail to thee
— O'er the sea,
— Fatherland.*

Koster (interrupting)

You're in the fatherland. That song is for when you're away.
(a pause.)

Lenz (brooding)

We *are* away. Is this the fatherland — torn with poverty and despair, without future, without hope?

Koster (soberly)

We didn't talk like that in 1918 when things were worse.

Lenz

We still believed. And now, we've stopped believing.
(pause)

* "Ubers Meer Grüss Ich Dich Heimatland," a popular German song of the period.

There's only work to make you forget that there's nothing
to work for.
                    (pause)
Work and an occasional bottle.

Koster

What do you think of that gloomy talk, young Bobby?
                    (Bobby, absorbed, doesn't answer)
Answer your superior officer!

Bobby (recollecting himself)

Excuse me. I must have a touch of Spring Fever.
                                        CUT TO:

41   A HUGE BUICK TOWN CAR —

            — drawing up and overtaking them. As it comes
            abreast, a hand appears momentarily in the window
            and discards a half-smoked cigarette, which lands
            with a shower of sparks in "Heinrich."
                                        CUT TO:

42   INTERIOR OF "HEINRICH"

            The cigarette falls in Bobby's lap; he starts and
            gropes for it.

Koster (muttering fiercely)

So you think you can pass our old Heinrich, do you?

Lenz

Little he knows that Heinrich has the great heart of a racer.
Take him, Otto.
            "Heinrich" has fallen a little behind the Buick —

now he steps on it and draws abreast again. We
see:

43   FOUR LIGHTS IN A ROW —

— the two crazy, patched eyes of "Heinrich," and
the big bright eyes of the Buick as they appear
at a distance in the twilight and RACE TOWARD
THE CAMERA.

Three times we see this, each time at a faster pace.
Once, two other cars approach from the two sides
of a crossroad, their lights stopping abruptly and
making a great blurr, through which plunge the
two racers.

CUT TO:

44   GLIMPSE OF THE COMRADES

Lenz's newspaper blown against his face.

CUT TO:

45   THE BUICK DRIVER'S FACE —

— set and annoyed as he pats the arm of an invisible
feminine companion at his side.

CUT TO:

46   "HEINRICH'S" LIGHTS —

— enlarging, drawing ahead and racing directly
toward us in victory.

DISSOLVE TO:

47   EXTERIOR A WAYSIDE INN —

— idyllic and vine-covered, built from an old water
mill. A stream still turns the wheel with a gentle,
splashing sound. Within the restaurant a mechani-

cal piano is playing "Goodbye My Dearest Guards Officer."

"Heinrich" snorts up, and the Comrades get out.

Koster (sniffing)

Liver and onions.

Lenz (gently laying his hand on the steaming radiator)

I think it's the gear-box.

Koster

Don't forget the drinks.

> As they take out the bottles, the Buick they passed pulls up and stops, and the man at the wheel steps out.
>
> Erich Breuer is about forty, a parvenu and a profiteer. He has modeled himself on the aristocrat, but the veneer is thin and the butcher boy is often in evidence, especially when he is angry or at a disadvantage. He wears a camel's hair coat, a monocle and yellow gloves which he pulls off as he looks angrily at the car that defeated him.
>
> Lenz and Bobby wear superior expressions.

Koster (in a low, warning voice)

Great Snakes! We don't want two fights today.

Breuer (addressing them)

What kind of a junk is that?

Lenz (coolly, after a moment's pause)

Did you say something?

Breuer (testily)

I asked what make it was.

Lenz (insolently)

Well, the grandpa was a sewing machine, the grandma was an old radio, and the pappa was a machine gun —
> (he breaks off)
> From the other side of the Buick there has appeared a lovely girl. Patricia Hollmann is in her middle twenties, stylish and beautiful — and something more. She seems to carry light and music with her — one should almost hear the music of the "Doll Dance" whenever she comes into the scene — and she moves through the chaos of the time with charm and brightness, even when there are only sad things to say.
>
> Seeing her, the Comrades suddenly change their attitude. She smiles and they smile back at her.

Breuer (not knowing what to say)

My name's Breuer.

Lenz (introducing)

Lenz — Koster — Lohkamp. Why don't you show Mr. Breuer the car, Otto?

Koster (very politely)

With pleasure.

Breuer (more pleasantly)

I'd like to see it. You wiped me off the map.
> Otto Koster and Breuer move toward "Heinrich."

Lenz and Bobby, struck by Pat's beauty, are a little shy.

Bobby

It's a lovely night.

Pat (quite at ease)

Gorgeous.

Bobby (embarrassed)

Unusually mild.

Lenz (very gravely)

Terribly mild.

> This doesn't sound quite right to him. He goes to join Koster and Breuer beside the car, leaving Bobby and Pat alone. They take a few steps so that the mill wheel, dripping water, revolves directly behind them. Pat is very slim, very lovely in the uncertain light from the inn; she is an English type, blonde, with silky brown hair, face narrow and pale, cheeks rather wan, long thin hands and big, bright, passionate eyes.

Bobby (admiringly)

We didn't know there was anyone so — you know — in the car. Or we'd have let you win.

Pat (her voice is slow, deep, exciting, slightly hoarse)

But why should you?

Bobby

It wasn't fair. We can do ninety-five.

Pat (whistles and puts her hands in her pockets)

Ninety-five!

Bobby

You couldn't know that, could you? I think Herr Breuer is annoyed.

Pat (shrugs her shoulders)

One ought to be able to lose sometimes.

Bobby (after a short pause)

Is that your husband you're with?

Pat

No. He's a friend. Are you three brothers?

Bobby (surprised)

No. Do we look alike?

Pat

Not exactly —
                    (looking at him)
— yet you have the same look — a very proud look.

Bobby (laughs)

We run a repair shop.
          Herr Breuer comes back enthusiastically into the
          scene, followed by Lenz and Koster.

Breuer

I don't mind losing now. Mr. Koster has been a speedway

racer — won the Grand Prize at Hamburg this year. I'm proud
that it was so close.

> (he laughs — cars are his hobby)

Mr. Koster and his friends are supping with us.

> (he claps Koster on the shoulder)

Hey, old man.

> DISSOLVE TO:

48   THE INTERIOR OF THE WAYSIDE INN —

> — rustic and cozy with a blazing fire. The turning
> mill is visible through the window, and the rushing
> stream is audible in the room. The party has fin-
> ished supper and is drinking wine. There are no
> other guests. Breuer, a little drunk and very talka-
> tive, sits beside Koster.

Breuer

Koster, when you take a curve at high speed, do you use
the brake or change gears?

Koster

I just turn the wheel.

> Breuer laughs as if that were an excellent joke.

Breuer

I drove a cab in the war — a staff car — in Berlin. It was
better than the front.

> (he laughs again. Koster nods tolerantly)
> Lenz and Bobby sit on either side of Pat. Bobby
> stares shyly, admiringly at Pat. Lenz is doing the
> "Floating Sugar Trick." (Details appended at end
> of script)

Lenz

Now — *sink!*

> (the floating cube of sugar sinks to the
> bottom of the cup)

Pat (friendly, not supercilious)
Extraordinary!

Lenz

Thank you, Madame.

> (he looks at her)

You know, this is a great event for us.

Pat (surprised)

To come here?

Lenz

To meet you.
>(he looks around)

Time has ceased to flow on for a minute — as if we'd stopped in a lovely pool.
>(he smiles)

You see, our lives are not very exciting.

Pat

You seem cheery enough.
>(looks at Bobby's bruise)

And pugnacious.

Lenz

Oh, we're that. We go armed. But when we meet someone like you we take off the armor.

Pat

You mean you're — political?

Lenz

Well — I have my sympathies — but Koster and young Bobby here keep out of it.
>(more intensely)

No — I was speaking of the struggle for existence in this country of ours.

Bobby (afraid this is too grave for such a shining lady)

I like the way you dress.
>The tension of Lenz's seriousness relaxes.

Pat

My only good costume. I feel very English in it — My mother was English. That's why I'm Patricia.

Bobby

Patricia.

Lenz

Pat. That's a fine name — easy to say. My name's Gottfried. His name is Bobby.
> (Bobby is a little awed by the familiarity)

He only tasted the war — he didn't get boiled very hard — he can still be saved.

Bobby (flustered)

What do you mean saved?

Lenz (staring straight ahead)

Saved for life —
> (the radio begins to play "Falling in Love Again." Lenz remembers something)

By Heavens, it's his birthday! Where's the rum?
> (he reaches for it and fills the glasses)

Pat (to Bobby)

How old?

Bobby (ruefully)

Thirty.

Pat (with an appraising provocative look)

That's a very fine age — thirty.

DISSOLVE TO:

49 EXTERIOR OF THE INN

Under an arbor, Bobby and Pat are walking toward the cars, followed by Koster, Breuer and Lenz. Bobby and Pat are silent — the other three are singing the "Song of the Argonnerwald." Bobby is carrying Pat's cloak. She looks up at the stars as she puts it on — her lips are slightly open in a smile. They reach the cars.

Bobby (attentive)

Do you think Herr Breuer is fit to drive?

Pat

I think so.

Bobby (anxiously)

If you're not quite sure, one of us could go with you.

Pat

It's all right. He drives better when he's had a little.

Bobby

But not so surely.
                    (prolonging the moment)
Let's hope he'll do all right. Can I phone you in the morning and see if you got home? We're responsible — with that birthday rum.
                    (the others come up. Breuer gets into the car)

Pat

All right, if you like. Western two seven nine six.
          She gets into the Buick. The Comrades bow and

wave as the Buick roars away. Bobby notes the phone number on a match packet.

Lenz

I wonder what she finds in that auto catalogue? Wonderful girl, oh?

Bobby (pretending indifference)

Who am I to say?

Lenz (teasingly)

What do you live for, Bobby?

Bobby (abstracted)

I've been asking myself that for a long time.

Lenz (with meaning)

Maybe I could tell you.
> (he gets into "Heinrich")
> Unobserved, Bobby leans over and pats "Heinrich."

Bobby (with feeling)

Thank you, Heinrich!

                                        FADE OUT

50   FADE IN:
            COURTYARD OF THE REPAIR SHOP —

— on a sunny morning. The radio in the office is playing "Tea for Two." The wrecked Ford is in process of reconstruction. Bobby takes his overalls from the plum tree in the yard, disclosing to his amazement that it has blossomed beautifully during the night. Matilda, broom in hand, stands beside him.

Bobby

Well, look at the old plum tree!

Matilda

Every Spring it's a fresh miracle. And the smell — just like rum —
>   (sniffs)
Fine old rum.
>   Jupp comes up to the tree and picks some blossoms.

Jupp (to Bobby)

Good morning.

Bobby (idly)

What's the idea?

Jupp

For the ladies. I give them a spray with each gallon of gas. Helps business.
>   (he retires)
>   Lenz's head appears from beneath the Ford. He lies on a creeper.

Lenz

Say, Bob, it's occurred to me that something ought to be done about that girl of Herr Breuer's.

Bobby (starting)

What do you mean?

Lenz

Just that. What are you glaring at me about?

Bobby

I'm not glaring.
                    (he puts on his overalls)

Lenz (crawling out, covered with grime)

You *are* glaring. What was her name? Pat what?

Bobby (after a pause)

How should I know?

Lenz (on his feet)

You wrote down her address — I saw you.

Bobby (quickly)

On a match packet — and I threw away the packet.

Lenz (seizing him by the hair)

Threw it away? After Otto and I spent an hour with Breuer
so you could make a hit. Threw it away? Holy Cats!
                    (considers)
Maybe Otto knows it.

Bobby

No he doesn't.

Lenz (wrathfully)

Of all the blasé infants! You twerp, you! Don't you know
that was a wonderful girl?

(ecstatically)

Let me tell you, she was manna from heaven. You didn't have the brains to appreciate her. Did you see those eyes? — of course not — you were looking at yourself in a glass of brandy.

Bobby (picks up a hand pump)

Oh, pipe down.

Lenz (tenderly)

And her hands — long and slender like Romaine salad — or endives —

Matilda (sweeping in the b.g.)

I declare, you make my mouth water.

Lenz

Otto and I understand such things. At last we find a perfect girl — not only beautiful, but with atmosphere —
(glaring at Bobby)
Do you know what atmosphere is, you low-lifer?

Bobby (working the hand pump)

Sure. The stuff that comes out of here.

Lenz (pityingly)

Atmosphere is radiance, glamour, warmth, mystery. It is what gives beauty a soul and makes it alive.

He is gesturing passionately. Suddenly he stops, his arms fall to his side.

CUT TO:

51   WHAT HE SEES:

PUPPI, THE INJURED BAKER, AND A TOUGH,
DUMPY WOMAN —

— who have come into the courtyard. Puppi wears
his arm in a sling. Matilda looks disapprovingly
at the woman.

Puppi

Good morning.
> (he looks at Bobby and Lenz and somehow
> his haughty manner fails in mid-speech)

Isn't my car ready?

Lenz (brought down to earth)

Your what? Your car — not quite. That was a terrible beating
you gave it. Another three days.
> (he turns indifferently to the Ford)
> A horn sounds and Koster, in the Cadillac, drives
> out of the work shop and stops momentarily beside
> the group.

Koster (to Puppi)

How-de-do.

Puppi

Say, I wish you could hurry up my car.

The Woman (looking admiringly at the Cadillac)

Is this it?

Koster

No. This one is sold. I'm going to deliver it now. But your
Ford will look like new when we're done with it.

Puppi (indicating the wreck to the woman)

That one's mine.

Woman (sniffishly)

O that. I thought you had a real car.

> Lenz is back under the car and Bobby has become absorbed in something he conceals in his hand. Taking advantage of this, Puppi breaks a big sprig from the plum tree, gives it to the woman and grasps her arm to leave. Only Matilda sees and sweeps them out with a haughty flourish of the broom.

CUT TO:

52 WHAT BOBBY IS LOOKING AT:
INSERT:
A BATTERED MATCH PACKET —

> — on which is written "Western 2796". The lines seem to wriggle like snakes or tongues of fire, as if it has been burning his pocket.

53 BOBBY —

> — starts at the illusion, then glances carefully at Lenz, and we FOLLOW HIM to the interior of the office. He hesitates, picks up the phone, turns off the radio — just as Lenz begins a terrific banging in the courtyard.

Bobby (lingeringly into the phone)

Atmosphere . . . I beg your pardon. Western two seven nine six.

> Bobby waits for the connection with a beatific smile. The banging dies away as we —

CUT TO:

54   A SWITCHBOARD —

          — with a white winged angel sitting at it.

Angel (sweetly)

One moment, please — I'll connect you with heaven.

                                        CUT TO:

55   THE PEARLY GATES

          St. Peter, the caretaker, sitting beside another
          switchboard.

St. Peter (cackling)

I think she's in.

                                        CUT TO:

56   BOBBY'S FACE —

          — still ecstatic, changing to human embarrassment
          as Pat's voice says:

Pat

Hello.

Bobby

Oh, hello.
                    (with an artificial laugh)
This is that man.

Pat (calmly)

What man?

Bobby (helplessly)

That man you met the other night.

Pat (gentle, husky)

I've met lots of men — on lots of other nights.

Bobby (frowning)

Well — I don't know exactly how to describe myself.

Pat (mischievous)

Must you?

Bobby

I'm one of the men who beat you.

Pat (pretending alarm)

Really? You must have the wrong woman.

Bobby

In our car, I mean.

Pat (remembering)

Oh-h-h. Of course —
                (with more enthusiasm)
— you're the one who was so upset about the state of the
nation.

Bobby

No — I was —

Pat

Then you must be the one who sang with Herr Breuer.

Bobby (very apologetic)

No. I —

Pat (as if thinking)

Was there another — ?
                    (she laughs and stops teasing)
Of course I remember you.

Bobby (hurriedly)

I wondered if you got home all right. Did you?

Pat

Let's see, did I? Why yes, here I am.

Bobby

That's fine. Well —
                    (in wild embarrassment)
— goodbye.

Pat

Did you call up to say that?

Bobby

No, we — we just weren't very busy.

Pat (gently ironic)

Oh, a compliment. Oddly enough I won't be busy next
Tuesday evening.

Bobby (now utterly confused)

That *is* funny.

(a forced laugh)

Well, goodbye.

Pat

Till Tuesday evening.

Bobby (automatically)

Till Tuesday evening. What?
> The phone is dead. He wriggles the receiver, and
> we —
>> CUT TO:

57   A SATYR, WHO HAS REPLACED THE ANGEL
AT THE SWITCHBOARD —

> — pulling out the plug with a sardonic expression.
>> CUT TO:

58   BOBBY —

> — frowns, then reconsidering, smiles with satis-
> faction, and puts the match packet carefully away,
> as the scene —
>> DISSOLVES TO:

59   ALFONS' BAR AND RESTAURANT —

> — a neighborhood place, plain but with a certain
> distinction. Some day rich people will "discover"
> it. Alfons, the proprietor, is not introduced at
> present, but is in sight behind the bar.

> The Comrades are drinking. Bobby wears his best
> clothes, not very good ones, and is drinking for
> confidence. Lenz has a strip of adhesive tape on
> his face.

Lenz (heatedly)

The country's mad. Little kids in soldier suits strutting around shrieking that they represent the Fatherland.

Koster

You let it come too near, you, Gottfried. Don't do that.
(pause)
There's nothing to hold on to right now. Things are rushing along like a stream of water.
(to Bobby)
What's more important is why Bobby's disguised like a gigolo.

Lenz (feeling Bobby's new tie)

A big date, eh? Who is it?

Koster

Why shouldn't he have a date? Go to it, Bob, you're just ripe for love.

Lenz

He has the necessary simplicity.

Koster (defending Bobby)

Keep it. It's a gift of God that if you lose, you never get back.

Lenz (cynically)

Don't let it get you down, Baby — you can't help being born simple; just don't *die* simple.

Koster

He's envious, Bobby. He's really the last of the romantics, but he's afraid of the front line.
>   (enthusiastically)

Walk into it, Bobby. Remember — Parsifal was stupid — or he wouldn't have won the Holy Grail.

Bobby

Go on — ride me.

Lenz (remorseful)

We're not riding you. In bad times, simplicity is priceless.
>   (lightly)

A mature mind, mine for instance —
>   (he winks)

— sees too many obstacles and gets uncertain before it starts. Knowledge may make you free but it certainly doesn't make you happy.

Koster (raising his glass)

Here's to simplicity and all that goes with it, love and faith in the future, the dream of happiness, paradise regained.
>   (he drinks)

Bobby, we'll be with you in spirit.
>   The radio is playing "Falling in Love Again" as we

>   DISSOLVE TO:

60   THE HALL OF AN APARTMENT HOUSE

>   *(The following scene is an attempt to suggest the feeling of a rather shy young man calling on a girl.)*

Bobby walks with leaden, slow-motion steps into

the elevator. To his alarm, it instantly whisks upward with a roar — almost as its gates close they
open again to eject him. He casts a reproachful
look at the elevator boy. Must he continue? Unseen
hands seem to push him from behind, so that he
leans backward in protest against the shoving. But
the door opens even as he presses the bell and,
following a maid, he is shoved like lightning along
a hall. The hands seem to leave him, and he stands,
limp, inside.

61   PAT'S APARTMENT

— small but furnished with remnants of magnifi-
cence. Portraits of generals and courtiers, a soft
carpet, cozy little armchairs in faded satin, rolling
tea table with tiny sandwiches, cakes and cocktail
shaker. A small radio plays a tinkling minuet. Pat
is standing to receive him.

Pat (very natural and gracious)

How do you do, Mr. Bobby.

Bobby

Well, am I the right man?

Pat (laughing)

That remains to be seen. Have a cocktail?

Bobby

Thanks.
                    (as she pours, he looks around)
This room is like something in a play.

Pat (offering a tray)

Canape?

Bobby (takes one)

Thanks. If I drop anything, remember I'm used to eating off of newspapers at the repair shop. I thought you told me you were poor.

Pat

I am. I'm living beyond my means.
> They drink.

Bobby

That was good. Felt warm.

Pat (gravely)

Then it's a good time to tell you the truth — I've got to leave you by nine o'clock.

Bobby (disappointed)

By nine?

Pat

Unfortunately. I only found out about it a few minutes ago, and I didn't know your address. It's a sort of business affair. I'm trying to get a job.
> (he looks at her cynically)

So shall we go right away?
> She takes his arm and they go down the hall.
>   DISSOLVE TO:

THE STREET OUTSIDE PAT'S APARTMENT —
TWILIGHT

A decayed, once-fashionable quarter. They turn
down the street.

Pat (breathing deeply)

I'm always so glad coming out that door. There was a time
I thought I would never leave that apartment again.

Bobby

How was that?

Pat (evasively)

I had to stay in bed. There wasn't so much to eat right after
the war, you know. I grew too fast and ate too little.

Bobby

How long were you in bed?

Pat

A year, but it seems a lifetime.
                They come to a tea room at the corner of the street.

Bobby (stopping)

How about this place?

Pat

It looks a little — stodgy, doesn't it?
                Bobby realizes she is used to the best and feels
                rather miserable.

Bobby

This was probably a mistake.

Pat

What do you mean?

Bobby

I mean I ought to take you —

Pat

Take me where you go.

Bobby

Oh, no! I go to Alfons' bar — but it's rough. No place for a girl like you.

Pat

It's just exactly the place for a girl like me.
                    (looking doubtful, he signals a taxi)
I'm really very easily pleased — very superficial and frivolous.
                    (a taxi stops and they get in.)
                                                  CUT TO:

63   INT. OF TAXI

Pat

When I got out of bed, I decided to live as I liked, even if only for a little while.

Bobby

Why not?

Pat

Everyone said I was a fool — that I ought to save my money and go to work. I wanted to be very gay and very irresponsible — and I was.

Bobby (fascinated)

I think it was a brave decision.

Pat (remembering)

Ach! I was frightened enough some times — as if I was in the wrong seat at the theatre. But it's all over now.

Bobby

When do you go to work?

Pat

In a week. Then I'll be too tired to go out in the evening.
                    (their eyes meet. It is a challenge, but quiet,
                    almost careless. Bobby responds.)

Bobby

That doesn't leave us much time.

                                                    CUT TO:

64   EXTERIOR ALFONS' CAFE

            They get out of the taxi.

Bobby (to newsboy at the door)

Mr. Koster and Mr. Lenz have left, haven't they?

Newsboy

Oh yes.

Bobby

Good.
> (to Pat)

All right — come on in.

Pat

What's the matter?

Bobby

Two especially tough men I didn't want you to see, that's
all.
> (they go in)

>> CUT TO:

65   INTERIOR ALFONS' CAFE

> They go through the crowded restaurant where
> several people salute Bobby. Four tarts at a table
> start to do likewise but refrain when they see Pat.
> They exchange winks. Bobby and Pat sit down in
> an alcove. Alfons, a huge gorilla of a man with
> sleeves rolled high on hairy arms, approaches them.

Bobby

A double whiskey, Alfons, and something to eat.

Pat (smiling)

I'll have a cocktail.

Alfons (he likes Pat)

We have Bavarian sausage and sauerkraut, milady.

Bobby (to Pat)

All right?
>   (Pat nods)
>   (to Alfons)

Fine.
>   (Alfons goes)

Pat (looking around)

I love this place. Do you come here often?

Bobby

It's our headquarters. The only trouble is the (lowers his voice) — choir singing.
>   Alfons reappears and puts down the drinks.

Alfons (to Pat)

Do you like choir singing?

Bobby

We love choir singing.
>   Bobby downs his drink as Alfons puts a record
>   on the phonograph and a male choir wheezes out
>   "Silence in the Forest."

Bobby

Another double.
>   Alfons, helped by a waiter, serves two steaming
>   plates of sausages.

Alfons (to Pat)

You look as if you loved good singing.

Pat (playing up)

Only choirs.

Alfons (interested)

Now that's funny. I do too.

66   EXTERIOR OF ALFONS' CAFE

Lenz and Koster.

Lenz (to newsboy)

Seen Mr. Lohkamp tonight?

Newsboy

Yes, sir. He's inside.

Lenz

Oh he is — is he?

Newsboy

He asked if you were inside and when I said no, he went in.

Koster and Lenz exchange a surprised glance and go in.

CUT TO:

67   INTERIOR OF ALFONS' CAFE — BOBBY AND PAT

Bobby (with feeling)

I never realized before what a fine place this is.

Pat

It *is* cozy.

Bobby (lowering his voice)

We're in a sort of dugout — shells are screaming overhead but they can't touch us.

Pat (falling into the play)

Are you sure?

Bobby

Yes —

(he looks at her gravely)

I don't know exactly why, but for some reason you and I are safe.

Pat

For the present.

Bobby

That's all you can ever ask in a war.

Pat (curious)

Are we in a war?

Bobby

My friends and I have found life to be a war.

Pat (thoughtfully)

You are very fond of each other, aren't you?
　　　The voices of Lenz and Koster from out of sight:

Lenz & Koster (o.s.)

Why, you two-faced liar, you hypocrite, you low heel! You
snake in the grass, you fresh punk, you baby-faced double-
crosser!
　　　PAN TO LENZ AND KOSTER, drawing up chairs.

Pat (laughing)

Why, hello. Do sit down.

Lenz (icily)

We wondered if you got home safely last week, but our
friend —
　　　　　(ironic emphasis on the word)
— lost the address.

Bobby

I only had the phone number.

Koster (ignoring him)

You got home safely?

Pat (laughs)

Herr Breuer knocked over a lamppost but it didn't matter.
There are lots more.

Koster

Waiter, some — . What are you drinking? Let's have the
same. You see, Pat, we three share everything.

Pat

I hope that includes me —
                    (she looks at her watch)
— but only till nine o'clock. I don't want to keep Herr Breuer
waiting.

Bobby (suddenly blue)

Oh, waiter — another double whiskey.
                    (he looks at his plate and says ruefully)
Some delicacies come in very thin slices.
                                        DISSOLVE TO:

68   EXTERIOR PAT'S DOOR

          The elevator waits — the boy looks at Pat and
          Bobby from the cage.

Bobby (rather stiffly)

I can't help hoping you won't combine business — with pleasure.

> Momentarily surprised, Pat stares at him. Then getting his meaning, she suddenly laughs.

Pat

You baby. Good heavens, what a baby you are!

Bobby (blunderingly)

Well, if you — anyway — you think I'm a halfwit.

Pat (gently)

No, I don't.

> (she looks at the elevator boy and points for him to go down)

The gentleman can walk.

> The elevator boy nods. As he goes down, Pat suddenly comes into Bobby's arms — a kiss, complete but only one, and she is gone.

> DISSOLVE TO:

69   EXTERIOR BOBBY'S BOARDING HOUSE

> — a three-story house that has seen better days. Bobby enters.

70   BOBBY ON A FLIGHT OF DREARY, UNCARPETED STAIRS

> Near the top he suddenly starts back as if at an apparition.

> CUT TO:

Hasse, a poor accountant, a drooping, beaten little man, has run out of his room onto the landing. He is followed by a stream of feminine abuse.

Woman's Voice

— and stay out, you little rat. Us move to a cheaper room! Never! Not on your life! What could be worse than this one? Ach! What a husband!

    The door bangs.

Hasse (explaining desolately to Bobby)

I want to move only because I'm afraid — I'm afraid. Two more men were fired from the office today — I'll be next, see if I'm not.

Bobby (a little tight)

Cheer up, Herr Hasse.

Hasse

I work overtime every night and always these reproaches.

Bobby

You ought to beat her — or else take her to the movies. Take her to a loving movie. Let her dream.

Hasse (bitterly)

You're lucky to be alone.

Bobby (seriously)

Do you think it's fun to be alone? That's no good either — take it from me.

The sound of a glass breaking within the room. Bobby has an impulse and goes back downstairs.

CUT TO:

72   CORRIDOR BELOW

Several doors are opened suspiciously. From one peeks the head of Frau Zalewska, the landlady.

Frau Zalewska

Good evening, Mr. Lohkamp.

The heads of other boarders peer out as Bobby goes along the lower corridor toward the phone. He takes up the receiver.

Bobby

Western two seven nine six.

The heads regard him. When he looks at one, it disappears, but another pops out across from it, so that his own head jerks from side to side spotting them. There are some coats hanging beside the phone. He makes a sort of tent of them and puts the phone inside.

Bobby

Hello.

Pat's Voice

Oh, hello.

Bobby

Having the business interview?

Pat's Voice

It's all over. I'm on my way to bed — a bit feverish.

Bobby

I'm sorry.
> (he pushes aside the coats and takes a
> breath of cool air)

You never heard the name Robert before, did you?

Pat's Voice (sleepily)

Yes.

Bobby

Let's hear you pronounce it. Say "Robert is terrific".

Pat's Voice (laughing)

Robert is a baby. And I like him that way.

Bobby

Now try "Bob". "Bob is a —"

Pat's Voice (softly, slowly)

Bob drinks too much. Now, I've got to hang up — I've taken a sleeping pill.

Bobby

Goodnight — sleep well.
                              CUT TO:

73   INTERIOR PAT'S APARTMENT

> Pat, full dressed and wide awake, hangs up the

phone and stretches out on the couch, smoking.
Herr Breuer is lounging familiarly in a chair.

Herr Breuer (irritated)

He has his nerve.

Pat

He's just a boy.
                    (Breuer looks at her narrowly)

Breuer

Your taste seems to be deteriorating.

Pat (pointedly)

When one has left one's own world, people are much the
same.
                    (Breuer takes this hard)

Breuer

You haven't answered about the phonograph shop.

Pat

I'd like it.
                    (smiling to herself)
I could sell records of choirs.

Breuer (puzzled)

What do you mean?

Pat

I was just thinking of something.

(her expression changes)

But I won't take that ridiculous salary. I'll take a commission, that's all.

Breuer (earnestly)

Pat, I want to help you. It'd be a year before a shop would pay you enough to live on.

Pat (carelessly)

Then let it go. I'm sorry. I've thought it over, and I don't want anything that way. Pour me some more champagne.

DISSOLVE TO:

74   THE COURTYARD OF THE REPAIR SHOP
       NEXT MORNING

Seated in the repaired Ford are Puppi, the baker, and his girl-friend. Puppi is counting out money to Koster who stands in overalls beside the car.

Koster

You'll find it's better than ever.

Puppi's Woman (sullenly)

That's not saying much.
                    (she nudges Puppi)
Ask him about that other car.

Puppi (unwillingly)

My fiancee thinks she likes that other car you had — that Cadillac.

Koster

I told you, it's sold and delivered.

Puppi's Woman (very disappointed)

That was really a refined car.

Koster (calculating the strength of her desire)

Maybe the man who bought it will sell it. We could call him up.
>   (raising his voice)

Hey, Bobby!
>   (he looks around)

He was here a minute ago.
>   THE CAMERA MOVES TO SHOW BOBBY, un-
>   seen by the others, asleep in the back seat of the
>   Ford. He has a hangover and his hands press a
>   piece of dirty waste against one side of his head,
>   an oil can against the other.

Puppi (wanting to drop the subject of the Cadillac)

Never mind. I'm sure it would be too expensive.
>   He starts the engine, violently awakening Bobby
>   who, in a nightmare, jumps up and raises the oil
>   can as if to bean Puppi. He recovers himself.

Koster

Bobby, you're a persuasive fellow.

Bobby (yelling — still dazed)

What?

Koster

Do you think we could buy back that Cadillac?
>   (he winks)

The lady has taken a fancy to it.

Puppi

No she hasn't, really.

Bobby (perking up)

Let me try to get back the Cadillac.
                    (to the woman)
It certainly would become you better than this.
                    The woman, beaming, throws her arms around
                    Puppi's neck.

The Woman

Oh, sweetheart.

Koster (thoughtfully)

He might sell for seven thousand marks —

Puppi (starts his car rolling slowly)

Ach, that would be suicide!

Bobby (running along beside)

We'd take this off your hands.

Puppi

Never.

Bobby (sprinting)

A car fit for a queen — I'll find out.
                    As the car passes through the gate, Bobby is
                    stopped sharply by the fence, but his excitement
                    remains.

                                        DISSOLVE TO:

75   INTERIOR OF THE OFFICE

Bobby is hanging up the phone. Koster listening.

Bobby (excitedly to Koster)

He'll sell — for six thousand marks. Five hundred more profit for us.

Koster (jubilant)

We've got the landlord stopped this month. Rags to riches in a week.

> Bobby starts to dance — then groans and sinks down in a chair with his hand on his head. Koster pours himself a drink and offers the bottle to Bobby.

Bobby (shaking his head)

I'm fed up with this damned boozing.

Koster

Just as well.

Bobby (after a pause)

Say, Otto, you've been all over the world — South America and everything —

> (he indicates a picture of a beautiful dancing Senorita on the phone table)

— tell me this. Does a man in love always behave like a sucker?

Koster

Always.
> (pause)

The whole thing is a racket — mother nature's favorite racket.

(points out the window)

It's like that plum tree — making itself more beautiful than it ever will be again. Love is a swindle — it couldn't be put over on the square.

Bobby

Do people in love always make fools of themselves?

Koster

A man can't make a fool of himself in a woman's eyes by anything he does for her sake. Do anything you like — turn cartwheels for her, dress up like Santa Claus, write her a poem in Chinese, pass out on her doorstep — only one thing to avoid —

Lenz (his voice only)

Don't — ever — make — sense.

They jump, and the CAMERA MOVES to show Lenz looking in a window.

Bobby (to Lenz)

Did you ever take a girl out and get drunk?

Lenz

Often.

(looks knowingly at Bobby)

Did you act very cute last night? Well, don't apologize. Send flowers. Only flowers. They cover up everything.

(with his usual touch of cynicism)

Even graves.

DISSOLVE TO:

76   A STREET — BOBBY

standing beside "Heinrich", looking covetously
over a wall at a lilac tree — then stealthily helping
himself.

DISSOLVE TO:

77   THE LILAC BRANCH

held in Pat's arm as they roll along the streets of
the city. Evening. The lights shining.

Pat (dreamily)

Wonderful air. It smells of spring.

Bobby

We can go out into the country.
(Pat shivers)
Are you cold?
(she turns up her collar and tucks her hands
in her coat pockets)
Your dress is too light.

Pat (shakes her head)

I don't like heavy things. It'll be nice when it's really warm
this Summer.
(he spreads a robe over her lap)
Cold makes you miserable.

Bobby (solicitously)

Would it make you warm to drive?

Pat

I don't know how.

Bobby (surprised)

You can't drive?

Pat (shakes her head)

And once we had three cars.

Bobby (looking straight ahead)

Herr Breuer might have taught you.

Pat

He likes girls to be helpless.

Bobby (critical)

He would.

Pat (dreaming)

If I had a car, I'd drive about the streets every evening —
half awake, half dreaming. Then one wouldn't need anyone
else.

Bobby (thoughtful)

You do need someone — in the evening.

Pat

Yes. It's odd — when it turns dark you need someone.

Bobby (moved)

Let me teach you to drive.

DISSOLVE TO:

THE COUNTRYSIDE —

— white with moonlight. The engine off. The shrilling of frogs.

Bobby (practical)

— Now, we'll start from the beginning again. First the ignition — a sort of spark —

Pat (with meaning)

Everything starts with a spark.
                    (she starts the car running)

Bobby (indicating the directions)

Remember — first speed — second speed — third speed.
          She goes into first speed. The car moves.

Pat (frightened)

Heavens! It's actually going!

Bobby

First speed is the strongest.

Pat

And the safest?

Bobby

Not always. Now, second speed.
                    (a screech as he leans forward; his arm has
                    gone around her)
No, always the clutch.

Pat (laughing as his arm presses her)

Always the clutch — for all speed.

Bobby

Now third — the fastest.
                    The car slows up.

Pat (appalled)

What have I done?

Bobby

It's in neutral.

Pat

How uninteresting.
                    (with meaning)
I don't like neutral.

Bobby (getting it)

Neither do I.
                        (he leans toward her but at that moment,
                        before the car quite stops, she gets it in
                        third and they go forward. He cautions her)
Not too fast.

Pat

What happens if you're caught?

Bobby

No license. You'd go to jail.

Pat (laughing)

The woman pays. Even in a car.

Bobby (sentimental)

But even in a car — there's always some place where it's light and warm.

CUT TO:

79   CLOSE SHOT. THE LITTLE AREA AROUND THE DASHBOARD.

Their hands just touching.

DISSOLVE TO:

80   THEIR HANDS OVER A TABLE —

— in Alfons' Cafe, later in the night. Another gay night, with music and a friendly crowd at the tables. Alfons behind the bar and superintending supper.

Bobby (romancing)

— then I batted around the world on freighters — especially South America.

Pat

I've always wanted to go to South America.

Bobby (thinking hard)

Well, there's Rio de Janiero — and Buenos Aires.

Pat (expectantly)

Yes?

Bobby (inventing)

You roll down to Rio. It's wonderful. Then — then you roll down to Buenos Aires. They have monkeys — no, they have coffee. Monkeys and coffee.

Pat (mock serious)

All rolling around, I suppose. Did you stay there long?

Bobby

Oh yes — years. Mostly in Rio de Jan —

Pat (interrupting)

I know — and Buenos Aires. I mean, did you go up the Amazon?

Bobby

There weren't any Amazons. There was mostly coffee —

Pat

And monkeys.

Bobby (fascinated with himself)

Yes. Monkeys and coffee. A big harbor and the cities white and high above it, and crocodiles and jaguars and orchids growing in the darkness —
> (he stops, suddenly ashamed of his roman-
> tics. The radio is playing)

That's a new American tune . . . it's called "I Can't Give You Anything But Love, Baby."

Pat

It's sort of sad. Tell me more about South America.

Bobby

Well —

> (he takes out Koster's picture of the Señorita which he has purloined from the frame in the garage, and hands it across the table; then suddenly he looks up to see Koster and Lenz standing beside them.)

Koster

I'd like to hear about South America, too.

Lenz

At last we know where he is every evening. Hello, Pat.

Koster

Has Bobby told you how he took us with him to South America?

Bobby (very flustered)

No, I —

Koster (seeing the picture)

Great Snakes! A live Señorita! What do you think of her, Gottfried?

Lenz (examining it)

Not bad — her chassis is sprung. Is this the one who sued you for breach of promise, Bobby?

Bobby

Now look here —

Koster

No, that's the one he married. Does she know you're out tonight, Bobby?

> Pat, amused, looks fondly at Bobby. Alfons comes
> up.

Alfons

A round of cocktails on the house — The Three Comrades — always together.

Pat

I'm afraid I'm — extra.

Koster

No, you're not. We welcome you. One and all, we approve of you.

Alfons

And what will you have in honor of this? Some pork chops?

Pat

Divine.

Alfons

Waiter, the chops!
> (to the group)
A wonderful pig — took two firsts.

> The waiter sets down a tray of drinks and shows
> a dish of raw chops.

Koster (gloating)

Very promising.

Alfons (raising his glass)

Pros't! To the new recruit — now an old soldier.
> Smiling, Pat drinks with the Three Comrades.
>> DISSOLVE TO:

81   INTERIOR ALFONS' CAFE

> — several hours later. Alfons is closing up. Pat and the Three Comrades are moving toward the door. False dawn has come up outside, making a blue oblong of the door; through which we see a procession of horse-drawn wagons and dog carts passing. The drivers are chanting a folk song:

"In Einem Kühlen Grunde" *

Bobby, Lenz and Pat

Goodnight, Alfons.

Koster

Good morning, rather. Those are the carts coming into market.

Lenz

Come on — we'll go to the market and buy all the flowers in the world.
> They run for the nearest wagon, one simply overflowing with piles of cut flowers. Koster and Lenz swing themselves up front with a good-natured peasant.

---

* "In a Cool Little Glade," F. Gluck. See book: *Volks-Kommers. Wanderlieder*, Hugo Hartman. Page 23.

Koster

Ten marks for a ride in your caravan.

> Bobby and Pat get in the rear of the wagon and
> lie back luxuriantly against the flowers. The tail-
> board is just high enough to hide them. Lenz, in
> front, throws a handful of flowers, which arches
> over the high heap and falls on them.

Bobby

You don't really love me, do you?

Pat (shaking her head)

No. Do you love me?

Bobby

No. Lucky, isn't it?

Pat

Very.

Bobby

Then nothing can hurt us.

Pat

Nothing.

Bobby

> (puts his arm around her with a passion
> that belies his words)

But you'd better not get lost in here, because I'd never be
able to pick you out from the other flowers.

> His arm around her — she lies closely to him.

Pat

I'm not this kind of flower. I'm afraid the hothouse variety.
                    (she picks up a blossom and addresses it
                    rather sadly)
I'd love to be like you, my dear.

Bobby (holding her close to him; passionately)

Oh you are — you are!
                    They lean far back into the flowers as the song
                    rises to a climax and stops. Then silence, broken
                    only by the sound of the horse's hoofs through the
                    half-darkness.
                    FADE OUT ON "ACT ONE"
                    (About the first third of the story)

82   FADE IN ON:
            AN EXECUTIVE'S OFFICE —

            — modern but not lavish. A map of the city is
            spread on the desk, and Herr Breuer is marking
            off with a crayon a district as big as several wards.
            Beside him stands a tough, brutal looking young
            man in semi-military garb.

Breuer

— From now on, then, I will be the unofficial mayor of this
district. Is that clear?

The Lieutenant

Yes, mein Herr.

Breuer

Anything of importance must be brought immediately to my
attention.

The Lieutenant

I understand, mein Herr. From now on the district will be run from this office — by and for our organization.

Breuer

And for Germany.

The Lieutenant (carelessly)

Oh yes, and for Germany.
> A secretary appears in the doorway.

The Secretary

I have Fraulein Hollmann on the phone, Herr Breuer.
> The Lieutenant salutes and departs. Breuer picks
> up his phone.

Breuer

Hello, Pat. You've been hard to find this week . . . . No, you can explain later . . . .
> (he stops smiling)

Can I see you tonight? . . . Then I shall be at the opera myself. Afterwards you and your friend will be my guests for supper.
> (he hangs up, frowning)

CUT TO:

83   BREUER'S FACE

> — above a white tie he is adjusting in the mirror.
> A butler is snapping a buckle on his smooth vest.

CUT TO:

84   A LARGE SAFETY PIN —

> — on a very gaping vest. This is upon Bobby who

is in his room, being valeted by Koster and Lenz.
There are open suitcases of clothes on the floor.

Lenz

No — we need that safety pin to keep his tie down at the
back.

Koster

I know a way to do that with string.
> (he finished pinning the vest and begins
> on the string)

Bobby

Won't it show?

Lenz

Not as long as you don't take your coat off. That's a point
I forgot to tell you. Always keep your coat on in the opera
— no matter how you hate the tenor.

Koster

Give us the coat.
> (he helps Bobby into his own dress coat,
> but it is too big)

Lenz

Awful! Try mine.
> (Lenz's coat is tight but passable)
Like a glove.

Bobby

It's tight under my arms. Can't reach my pockets.

Koster

That'll save you a lot of money.

Lenz

It's fine. In that crowd, you won't show.

Bobby (nervously)

I wish you were coming.

Lenz

There's just enough clothes for one complete swell. Money?
                    (he hands some banknotes to Bobby)

Bobby

I've got enough.
                    (he pushes the money away)
We may not have a good month so soon again.

Koster (fiercely)

I am your superior officer. Anyhow, we're going to race
Heinrich next week and make a fortune.
                    (he thrusts the money into Bobby's pocket
                    and speaks seriously)
It's quite right what you're doing, Bobby.

Bobby (pretended indifference)

I can't figure her out exactly — how she stands with — Herr
Breuer.

Koster

Does it worry you?

Bobby (lying)

Not a bit.

Koster

It shouldn't. And I envy you.

Bobby

Why?

Koster

Because nothing else is worth a dime.
                    (picking up an opera hat)
And this tops you off.
                    (he tries it)
The thing won't open. Got a tire wrench?

Lenz

Bang it on something.
                    Koster tries that — on the electric light, which
                    explodes. But not the hat.

Koster

Never mind, Bobby. Carry it for the effect. It'll open when
it sees the other little hats.
                    (Bobby takes a last look and turns toward
                    the door)

Lenz

And don't forget to —

Koster

Let him alone. You've given him enough advice to last a year.

> Bobby winks at them and as a hand organ outside strikes up an old army song, "The Three Lilies," he goes out at a waiter's trot, carrying the opera hat like a tray on his fingers.

Lenz

Do you think it's wise?

Koster

Yes. It makes me happy that one of us at least has found —
> (he hesitates)

Lenz

Found what?

Koster

A window — to look back into the past, into what might have been.

Lenz

You need a drink. Bobby among the rich. I don't quite like it.

Koster

Pat's not rich.

Lenz

She is in her heart. I couldn't go to the opera while there

are shootings in the street every night. That's the sound in my ears.

Koster

Then for God's sake, let Bobby have his moment of happiness.

DISSOLVE TO:

85   INTERIOR.
            A NEW, SNAPPY-TAXI CAB

            — SHOOTING FROM the driver's seat at Pat, occupying the backseat alone. She wears a magnificient evening dress of silver brocade and sits pictorially with her arms stretched out to either side of the cab. Bobby is on the little seat with his knee visible and the unopened hat upon it.

Pat

Silly. Come back here.

Bobby

Of course I won't. I might rumple you. You look like a silver torch in this light.

Pat

That's what clothes are for.

Bobby

You need a richer man to match it.

Pat

The rich men I know are pretty awful, Bobby.

Bobby

If you say that often enough, I may got interested.
      The hat on his knee suddenly opens with a "Pop!"
      As Pat laughs, we —

                                              CUT TO:

86   TWO HANDS IN THE DARKNESS —

— lying along the arm of a theatre seat. SHOOT-
ING FROM BEHIND, through the interval between
the seats, we see them touch and then rise together,
back to back. The fingers intertwine and lock.

The curtain of the stage in front of them comes
down to end an act of *Tales From Hoffman.* The
music dies away, but the lights have not yet come
on. Behind a voice whispers:

The Usher (off scene)

Let me see your ticket stubs, please.

> Wonderingly, Bobby fumbles for them as the usher
> repeats the request to the pair at the end of the
> aisle — a plain German grocer and his fat wife.

Usher

Thank you. I'm sorry, but these seats were sold by mistake.
They are reserved for special customers.

The Grocer

What's that now?

Usher

The management requires these seats. You will get your
money back at the door.

> THE CAMERA PANS to a party of four waiting
> impatiently in the aisle.

CUT TO:

ROW OF SEATS

Bobby (angrily)

I won't move from here.

The Grocer (amid general turning of heads and murmurs of protest)

This is an outrage!
> The lights go on, showing that one of the party in the aisle is Breuer — very arrogant and unconcerned. The other man is a baldheaded oldster. With them are two richly dressed women.

Breuer (to the usher)

Hurry them, please.
> (suddenly he sees Pat and Bobby. Surprised, he changes his tone)

Not those two there — they are friends of ours. These.
> (he indicates two in front)

The Usher (to the two in front)

Let me see your stubs, please.

CUT TO:

88   THE GERMAN GROCER AND HIS WIFE —
> — going angrily up the aisle. Following them is another couple, an insignificant man and woman, humiliated and weepy.

The Grocer

Politics — that's it. New bullies in power.

CUT TO:

89   BREUER'S PARTY —

— seating themselves. Breuer leans across Bobby, who is frowning disgustedly, and speaks to Pat.

Breuer

I'm sorry you were accidently disturbed. We'll meet after the performance.

DISSOLVE TO:

90   THE EXTERIOR OF THE THEATRE —

— after the performance. There is a marked contrast between the wealthy opera patrons and the poverty-stricken crowd. Breuer's party is walking haughtily to the curb. Pat turns back to speak to Bobby, who has fallen a little behind.

Pat (with sympathy)

You're sad, darling.

Bobby

It was such fun — till he came.

Pat

He's just an old friend.

Bobby

That makes it worse.

Pat (gently)

Don't be silly.

Breuer (turning around)

I'm taking you to a new night club — that will especially
interest Pat.

> Unwillingly, Bobby gives in as we —
>>   DISSOLVE TO:

91   A NEON SIGN: "TRIANON"

> PAN DOWN TO a doorway in what looks like
> an elaborate private house. Breuer's party is getting
> out of the limousine.

> They stop as Breuer points with his cane to a coat
> of arms above the doorway. Pat gives a little cry.

Pat

It's our old house.
>   (shocked)
A night club!

Breuer

And a great success, I'm told.
> Pat recovers from her moment of shock and laughs.

Pat

I suppose I should be proud of that.
>>   CUT TO:

92   THE INTERIOR OF AN INTIMATE NIGHT-
            CLUB —

> — Cossack music — rhumbas and tangos rather than
> jazz — and a distinguished-looking clientele.

> The party sits down — Pat next to Breuer, Bobby
> between the two other women, thirtyish, rich, and

bejeweled, not quite "out of the top drawer." The
waiter takes the order.

Breuer (looking at the menu)

Champagne first? This Pol Roget, 1922?
　　　　　　　　(he looks around inquiringly)

Bobby

Some mineral water for me.

Pat (clapping her hands)

Bravo, Bobby.
　　　　　　At her evident interest in Bobby, Breuer's face
　　　　　　tightens a little.

Breuer (in a chilly voice)

And Appolonaris for — one.

Pat (looks around and shivers slightly)

This was the reception room. How often I've leaned over
those stairs and watched the dancing down below.
　　　　　　　　(ironically)
And now at last I can dance here myself.

Breuer

Will you?
　　　　　　They dance off, Bobby's eyes following. Frau
　　　　　　Schmidt, the woman at Bobby's side looks him
　　　　　　over lasciviously, wetting her lips.

Frau Schmidt

Are you an old friend of Erich Breuer's?

Bobby

Scarcely.

Frau Schmidt

He's become a man of influence. You saw how quickly he got seats in the theatre.

Bobby (ironically)

Yes.

        The waiter draws a champagne cork.

Frau Schmidt

He's very fond of Fraulein Hollman. And it's a lucky thing for her.
            (acidly)
These fallen aristocrats.
            (but rather impressed)
To think she used to live here!

93   OUT ON THE FLOOR —

     — Pat's cheek touches Breuer's. His arm tightens around the silver dress. He talks in a low, confident voice — sometimes she looks up at him and laughs.

94   BOBBY —

     — suddenly holds his glass out to the waiter pouring champagne.

Bobby

Include me.

95   FROM THE DANCE FLOOR — PAT —

         — looks at Bobby. She smiles encouragingly. For
         answer —

96   BOBBY —

         — raises the champagne glass to her gravely.

97   PAT —

         — opens her eyes as if saying, "Ahhh!" She and
         Breuer stop dancing and come back to the table.

Pat says her old house makes her dizzy. We'll drink and
move on.

         As they sit down —

                                      DISSOLVE TO:

98   ANOTHER NIGHT CLUB —

         — brighter and noisier. Breuer's party is gathered
         about a tank of live, swimming trout. A waiter
         brandishes a fish net.

Breuer

That fat one.

         The net goes in, the fish is captured.

Breuer (to Pat)

There's one the exact color of your dress.

Pat

Oh, which one?

Bobby

I hope he gets away.

Breuer

He won't. Catch him, there.
> (the fish manages to escape. The waiter goes
> after another)
> (testily)

No. I want that one.

Pat (suddenly comparing the fish to herself)

I don't. Oh, let it go — let it go!

Bobby (as it escapes again)

Poor little silver trout!
> Breuer meets Bobby's eye; aware of the symbolism
> of the episode, Breuer laughs contemptuously.
>> DISSOLVE TO:

99   THE TABLE — LATER

> The trout eaten. Breuer and Pat talking.

Breuer (lightly)

There's no reason why the Trianon Cabaret shouldn't become
a house again, if you chose.
> Bobby overhears this and stands up, facing away
> and taking a step toward the bar.

Frau Schmidt (a little drunk)

Where are you going, handsome?

Bobby

For a drink.

> She grabs at his coat-tail — this causes the back
> of his tie to jerk over his collar, revealing a length
> of string.

Frau Schmidt

Why, the man's all tied up in knots.

Bobby (politely savage)

I think I'd better go home — and get some more string.

Pat (alarmed)

I must go too — it's late.

Breuer

That's absurd. It's only one. We haven't started yet.

Bobby (quietly)

Can't you see she's tired?

Breuer (dryly)

You haven't known Pat as long as I have. She doesn't leave
parties early.
> (raises his eyebrows)
Why, my friend, you seem to be having trouble with your
shirt.

> Bobby looks at him angrily and seems about to
> blow up.

Breuer (to Pat)

This dance?

Pat

I have it with Bobby.

Bobby

Please excuse me. I'm not dancing.
                    (he bows frigidly, and Pat flinches)
                                        DISSOLVE TO:

100   THE INTERIOR OF THE LIMOUSINE —

           — on the way home. Pat half asleep between Breuer
           and Bobby. Bobby is sullen and silent.

Breuer

Where can I drop you?

Bobby

At the next corner.

Breuer

I'll gladly drive you home.

Bobby (looking out the window)

Drop me here at Alfons' Bar, if you please.

Breuer

Can you get in at this hour?

Bobby (ironically)

Thanks for your interest. I can get in.
                    (Breuer calls into the speaking tube. Bobby
                    touches Pat's hand)

I won't wake her. Goodnight, and thank you.
> (but as he shuts the door, she stirs)

Pat (half asleep)

Bobby — Bobby —

CUT TO:

101   INT. ALFONS' BAR — BOBBY —

> — sitting down with Lenz and Koster. They are surprised.

Koster

Hello — I thought you'd see the sun rise.

Bobby

I won't. Perhaps two other people will.

Koster

That man Breuer?

Bobby

About the worst twerp I ever met. Kicking people out of the theater to get himself a seat.

Koster

Alfons! Give Bobby a triple brandy, whiskey, gin and rum.

Lenz (disappointed)

She's a rich man's girl.

Bobby

Let's forget it. Tell me about the race at the speedway. What's the prize?

Koster

Five hundred marks cash.
                    (frowning)
Look here — don't quarrel with that girl — she's a thoroughbred.

Lenz (bitterly)

She's a rich man's girl. What can Bobby do? If he was an American like we read about, he could go out and get rich over-night. But here —

Koster

Forget it. Very few things will stand inspection at three o'clock in the morning.
                    Suddenly, Bobby raises his hand angrily and
                    smashes his glass.

Bobby (ashamed)

Sorry — I forgot where I was for a moment.
                                   DISSOLVE TO:

102   A DESERTED STREET

           Dawn is coming, dull smudges behind the house-
           tops. Bobby lurches along quite tight, his face pale
           and miserable. Reaching his house, he leans for
           a minute against the wall — then starts up the steps
           and searches for his key. In the dusk he hears a
           sound. Then he peers and sees a pale, indistinct

form, crouching on the steps. It is Pat, still in her
gleaming silver dress.

Bobby

Pat! Pat — what are you doing here?

Pat (stirring)

I believe I've been asleep.

Bobby

How did you get here?

Pat

I walked, darling.

Bobby

I mean why are you here at all?

Pat

I've been asking myself that for an hour.
                    (she stands up with a little fit of coughing)
Oh God, it's cold.

Bobby (sobering)

Pat, you're a marvelous girl, and I'm a damned idiot. But
you're shivering. Come inside here.
              With his arm around her, they go in.
                                        DISSOLVE TO:

103   BOBBY AND PAT —

              — entering his room, Pat exhausted from the climb.

He puts her on the bed and piles clothes on top
of her.

Bobby

Oh, how dumb I am! I should have called you from Alfons'.

Pat (sniffing)

Rum — cognac — whiskey — the League of Nations. Darling!

Bobby

I'm sorry.

Pat

Do you sleep on this bed?

Bobby

Yes — Oh, if I'd only known you were here. You're still
shivering.
                    (he piles more clothes on)
You're the first lovely thing that's ever been in this miserable
room.

Pat (sleepily)

You're pretty lovely yourself.
                    He draws up a low stool and sits down beside the
                    bed, leaning against it. Her eyes close.

Pat

You're a drunkard and a darling, and you didn't mean that
the other night.

Bobby

Mean what?

Pat

About not loving me.

Bobby (suppressing a desire to put his arms around her)

No, I didn't mean it.

> She closes her eyes; the birds are twittering outside
> the window. Bobby leans his elbow on the bed
> with his arm alongside hers. He yawns — his top
> hat opens with a dull thud.

DISSOLVE TO:

104   BREUER'S OFFICE — MORNING

> A few days later. Breuer at his desk, his lieutenant
> facing him.

Breuer

Did you make that little investigation?

Lieutenant

I did — the three of them own a sort of repair shop — a
poor little place. They pick up old jobs. You couldn't call
it a nest of revolutionaries, but one of them is — distinctly
dangerous.

Breuer (eagerly)

Which one? Robert Lohkamp?

Lieutenant

No. His name is Lenz. The other two don't seem to mix in politics.

Breuer (disappointed)

All right. Put this Lenz's name on our list. Where is this garage or shop?

Lieutenant (points it out on the map)

There — this corner.

Breuer (with meaning)

How very odd! We were thinking of establishing a club house or an armory in that vicinity. It might be just the spot, that corner. I'd like those men moved on.

Lieutenant

Where to?

Breuer

Where — I don't care.
                              (with sudden passion)
Out of Germany if necessary.

                                        DISSOLVE TO:

105   A RACE TRACK

           An enthusiastic crowd of racing fans.

           SHOOTING FROM THE GRANDSTAND
           ACROSS THE TRACK, we see eight cars pass in
           a flurry of dust, then CAMERA TRUCKS across
           track up to —

106   A LINE OF "PITS" ALONG THE BARRIER

Each bears a sign — "Deusenburg," "Renault,"
"Isotta-Fraschini," "Daimler," etc. We approach
the one marked "Heinrich," and find Pat, Bobby,
and Lenz all very excited, sitting on the barrier.
There are cans of oil piled within, and a spare set
of tires. Lenz is in mechanics' overalls and holding
a bottle of wine.

Lenz (tensely)

Otto's gaining — no he isn't. Come on, Heinrich! Good old
Heinrich. Last lap!

A Gigantic Mechanic (in the next pit)

What is that white junk? A trailer?

Lenz (truculently)

Who wants to know?
                    (the mechanic swells visibly)

Pat (warning him)

Don't, Gottfried. Hospitals are expensive.
               Lenz and the mechanic are interrupted by a yell
               of surprise from the crowd.
                                        CUT TO:

107   THE BACKSTRETCH

"HEINRICH" is creeping up on the others.
                                        CUT TO:

108 THE PITS

Lenz

He's stepping on it!

Bobby

Come on, Heinrich!

109 THE HOME STRETCH

The cars tearing for the finish. "Heinrich" and another are neck and neck — "Heinrich" sweeps by — to win.

CUT TO:

110 THE PITS

Lenz (to the big mechanic)

Yah! Yah!

Cheering from the crowd. But as the exhaust and dust blow into the pits, Pat has a violent fit of coughing.

Bobby (supporting her)

Are you all right?

Pat (choking)

Nothing — dust in my throat.

Lenz (excitedly hands her the bottle)

Try this!

(he rushes over to where Koster is stepping out of "Heinrich", surrounded by a crowd)

Pat

I haven't learned to drink from a bottle.
                    (coughing)
Isn't it fine we won, darling.

                                        DISSOLVE TO:

111   THE COURTYARD OF THE REPAIR SHOP.
             LATE AFTERNOON.

             The Comrades and Pat at the outdoor table by the
             plum tree, singing, "Wann die Soldaten Durch die
             Stadt Marschieren." *

             On the table sits the silver cup. "Heinrich" himself,
             with a wreath on his hood, stands in the back-
             ground.

             Jupp comes up to Lenz.

Jupp

There's a customer — only he doesn't seem like a customer.

Lenz

What? And we haven't anything to sell just now.
                    (he gets up)
Where is he?
                    (he follows Jupp)

Koster

Bobby, would you mind going along too?

Bobby (puzzled)

No — but why?

_____

* "When the Soldiers March through the Town." Hartman's Song Book.

Koster

Lenz might need you. Only for a minute, Bobby.
(Bobby goes — suspiciously)

Pat (touching the cup)

Was this worth risking your life for?

Koster (earnestly)

I'm going to do something more dangerous than that. Meddle in other people's business. How long have you known Bobby?

Pat

About six weeks.

Koster

Why don't you get married?

(Pat starts)

You love him, don't you?

(she doesn't answer)

He hasn't had much out of life.

(still she doesn't answer)

Think of all you could give him that he's never had.

Pat

It isn't that. it's — oh, it's this wretched body of mine.

Koster

It's an excellent body.

Pat

No — it's merely patched up. After the war, we didn't have enough to eat. I'm no good here.

(she puts her hand on her chest)

Koster

I guessed that.

Pat

I'm all right — when I take care of myself.

Koster

Let Bobby take care of you.

Pat

I wouldn't let anyone do that.

Koster

You little idiot — that's what he needs — something worthwhile to live for. That's what all this idle drinking is about. The world has somehow slipped away from Lenz and me — we don't want it to happen to Bobby.

Pat (shaking her head)

It doesn't make sense. Perhaps another kind of woman —

Koster

The kind he couldn't love?
Lenz and Bobby come back to the table.

Lenz (worried)

There seems to be some trouble about our license.

Koster

What is it?

Lenz

A fresh little squirt says we'll have to get it renewed. Or rather he said we could *try* to get it renewed.

Koster (scoffing)

What nonsense. We've been here two years. There'll be no difficulty.

Bobby

He said —

Koster

Sit down. You can go to the license bureau tomorrow.
(Lenz and Bobby sit down. Bobby next to Pat)

This evening is too important to spoil. Pat tells me she loves us all. Am I right, Pat?

Pat

You took the words out of my mouth.

Koster

But I want to resign in favor of Bobby.

Lenz

How about me? Bobby has that South American wife.

Bobby

Shut up, you grease spot.

Koster (pointing to the car)

Heinrich is all for it. He's rich now, and he offers to stake them to a week on the coast.
          Pat suddenly buries her head in Bobby's chest.

Pat

Darling, let me hide my blushes. You don't want a wife, do you?

Bobby (a little annoyed with Koster)

Will you let go my apron strings. Don't you think I can speak for myself?

Pat

Of course you can, darling —
                    (she raises her head)
— and let's hear you.

Bobby

Ladies and gentlemen —
> (he pauses, embarrassed, holding Pat in his
> arms)
— who is this woman?

Pat

Darling —
> (she looks up at him)
— it's just me.

Bobby

Oh.

Pat (looking into his eyes and imitating his tone.)

Oh.

> (he draws her closer. She speaks a little
> louder and very lovingly)

Oh!

> (then a little muffled as he holds her very
> closely)

Ohh.

> Koster and Lenz look at each other and raise their
> eyebrows reprovingly.

Koster and Lenz (as one would say "Aha")

O-oh!

DISSOLVE TO:

112   THE CORRIDOR OF A MUNICIPAL BUILDING

> A row of offices with information desks at intervals.
> Lenz, frowning, goes along the corridor, and stops
> at one, speaking to a clerk.

Lenz

My name is Lenz. Who is responsible for renewing business licenses?

Clerk

The License Bureau.

Lenz

There seems to be something funny about it. Our fees are paid, but I can't get the chief clerk's signature, and it's been three days.

Clerk

Not countersigned, perhaps.

Lenz

What's that?

Clerk

Something new.
                    (lowers his voice)
Everything now has to be O.K.'d by —
                    (he breaks off suddenly)
The Civil Service is down to the left.

Lenz

I didn't ask you —
                    At the sound of footsteps, he catches the clerk's
                    warning eye. Breuer's Lieutenant passes them,
                    going down the corridor.

Lenz

Oh, politics, eh? Something higher than the law. I wish I knew some of those boys.

> His glance falls across the corridor to the door from which the man has issued. THE CAMERA MOVES ALONG WITH HIS EYES to a glass door, on which is lettered:
> "ERICH BREUER Private Dept. of Appropriations"

Lenz's Voice (excitedly)

By heaven! I've met that gentleman.

Clerk

If you know Herr Breuer, it should be easy to arrange. He is not exactly *in* the administration, but —

> (he pauses significantly)
> Lenz has started for the office. He reconsiders and dashes for the pay telephone booth in the corridor.

Lenz

Western two seven nine six.

CUT TO:

113   CORRIDOR. BREUER'S LIEUTENANT

> — coming back carrying papers. He pauses at the desk.

Lieutenant

That man who was here — had he just been to the License Bureau?

Clerk

Yes. He's —

Lieutenant (interrupting)

Was his name Lenz?

Clerk

Yes.

> (he points to the phone booth)
> The lieutenant nods, smiles and goes on into Breuer's office.

CUT TO:

114   LENZ AT PHONE

Lenz

— but what luck! I remembered that he's a friend of yours. A word from you ought to fix it for us.

CUT TO:

115   PAT AT THE PHONE IN HER ROOM

> She has on her hat and is dressed to go out. She frowns a little.

Pat

I'll see him this morning. Goodbye, Gottfried.

> She hangs up, puts her face in a bowl of flowers with a card, "Bobby," beside it, picks up her bag and goes out.

DISSOLVE TO:

BREUER'S OFFICE.

Breuer behind his desk. Pat sitting upon it, smoking a cigarette.

Pat

— So you be a good fellow. Just tell all the little boys to let my friends alone.

Breuer (frowning)

It's not so simple as all that.

Pat (surprised)

What? You've told me often that you were on the inside.

Breuer

Who are these friends of yours?

Pat

You've met them.

Breuer (contemptuously)

Garage mechanics. This Bobby Lohkamp is no friend for you. And that Lenz — he's a mischief-maker, a firebrand.

Pat

Gottfried is?

Breuer (savagely)

Yes. He's headed for trouble. But the man I'm interested in, or rather *you're* interested in is Herr Bobby.
                    (his thin veneer of manners cracks)
And so I should go to a lot of trouble to help him.

Pat (coolly)

Certainly not, Erich.
                    (she gets up)
I forgot a lot of things about you for a minute. And thought of you only as a friend. Awfully silly of me.

Breuer

Look here — are you crazy about this fellow?

Pat

Crazy? That's a big word.

Breuer

Have you taken up with him?

Pat

Taken up what? Chess?
                    (she moves toward the door)

Breuer

You know I'd marry you tomorrow.

Pat

Not if I was married already.

Breuer

My God! Are you?

Pat

If those men were hounded out of their shop I think I'd be married that day.

Breuer (wiping his forehead in relief)

But not yet?

Pat

Not — yet.
                        (she opens the door and goes out)

Breuer (starting after her)

Pat!
            Angrily ringing a bell, he picks up a small bust
            of Napoleon from his desk and flings it from him.
            It just misses the head of his lieutenant coming
            in.

Lieutenant

You rang, Herr Breuer?

Breuer

I want a close watch kept on these people — a special investigation — day and night — Miss Patricia Hollmann, Otto
Koster, Bobby Lohkamp —

                        DISSOLVE TO:

117   AN AUCTIONEER'S YARD

            — full of old junk, furniture, books, etc. In the
            foreground, under the "AUCTION" sign, a bat-
            tered old taxi. Its owner, a Jew of about forty, thin
            and miserable, stands beside the auctioneer. In
            front of the bidders Pat and Koster sit on old chairs.
            Bobby and Lenz stand behind them.

Koster (addressing Pat and indicating the taxi)

That — if we get it — is going to carry you away on your honeymoon. That's its first job.

Pat

But we're not getting married.

Lenz

I still don't see why they want me along.
                    (he looks at Bobby)

Bobby

Don't look at me — I'm merely the fiancee.
                    THE CAMERA PANS SIDEWAYS to include a
                    Secretive Little Man with his eyes on our friends.
                    He is Breuer's investigator. Hold it to show that
                    he is straining to hear what they say.

A Voice (from the crowd)

Three hundred marks for the taxi.
                                        CUT BACK TO:

118   THE BIDDERS

Koster

Four hundred.

Auctioneer

Come, come. The taxi has its pride.

A bidder

Five hundred.

Koster

Seven-fifty.

Lenz (warning him)

Hey, Otto — that's our capital.

Koster

It's a great investment. And look at the poor devil who owns it! It would bring a thousand in better times.

Auctioneer

Seven-fifty — seven-fifty. Sold! This magnificent property to this gentleman.

> Koster and the others move forward. The spy melts away into the crowd.

Koster (introducing Pat to the taxi)

Your magic carpet.

Pat

Close up the repair shop, Otto, and we'll all go to the beach.

Koster

Impossible. One of us must stay.
> (CAMERA PANS to include taxi-driver, tears running from his eyes, as he gives his darling a last polish with a piece of waste)

Never mind, old fellow. We'll take good care of it.

Taxi Man

It's a fine car. Three years and never a breakdown. But I've been ill —

(he straightens his shoulders)

I should not complain but thank God for my blessings.

(almost with exaltation)

Here is one country where a Jew is not homeless — where the Fatherland belongs to him as well as to the others. For that I am proud and happy.

HOLD THE CAMERA on him for a moment to impress the false prophecy of these words then —
FADE OUT.

119   FADE IN ON:
THE OLD TAXI

— chugging along a country road. Bobby at the wheel. Pat beside him; Lenz asleep in the back seat on their piled suitcases.

Bobby (eyes on the road)

What does the meter read?

Pat (leaning forward)

Nine hundred and eighty marks.

Bobby

I hope you have the money, lady, or I'll have run you straight to the police station.

Pat

Sir, I can't give you anything but love.

Bobby

It won't buy gasoline.

Pat (wickedly)

Oh yes it will. They tell me it'll buy trips to the shore — look!

> (she points forward eagerly)
> SHOOTING FROM THE CAR, we see the road come to a hill-top, dip — and suddenly we are looking down at a wide panorama of beach and sea.

Bobby and Pat (turning excitedly)

Gottfried! Gottfried! The sea — the sea!

Lenz (awakening with a start)

See what?

> DISSOLVE TO:

120   THE BEACH — LATE AFTERNOON

> A circular bay, with a distant shore-line. On a hillock, about fifty yards back from the water, stands the Blue-White Inn, a simple little chalet. The beach is quiet; two little tents are pitched near the hull of a wrecked freighter, rotting on the sand.

121   CLOSEUP OF A TRAIL OF FOOTPRINTS

> Two pairs parallel in the sand. The sound of a man whistling, and we PULL BACK to show Lenz in an old-fashioned, knee-length, short-sleeved bathing suit, such as were still worn in Germany in 1928. He follows the footprints toward the sea, where they disappear around the corner of the freighter.
>
> Still whistling, he changes his course and walks

toward a little bathing tent where two children are playing.

CUT TO:

122 OTHER SIDE OF THE BOAT, LOOKING SHOREWARD

Disclosed are Pat and Bobby leaning against the hull. Pat, wearing a chic bathing suit, is rubbing oil on Bobby's shoulders. A handful of wild anemones are scattered in her lap. Bobby, like Lenz, wears a patched old-fashioned costume.

Bobby

Do you think that was Gottfried whistling?

Pat

I don't think. I don't think about anything — except about us and the sun and the holiday and the sea.

(she tickles his nose with an anemone)

Bobby

Take away your rose, woman.

Pat

It isn't a rose.

Bobby

Violet, then.

Pat

Isn't a violet.

Bobby

Then a lily — it better be — those are the only names I know.

Pat

Not really?

Bobby

I've always got by with those three. More oil.

Pat

No more. You just like the rubbing.

Bobby

Lazy mudfish. That's what you were fifty thousand years ago.

Pat

I still am a lazy mudfish. Not a very good play-fellow.

Bobby (fervidly)

But an extraordinary sweetheart.

Pat (sighing)

Not that either — just a sort of — fragment.

Bobby

A lovely fragment. I'd get very weary if you were perfect. But a lovely fragment — darling. I'll love you forever.

                                        CUT TO:

123   THE LITTLE BATHING TENT

> Lenz sitting in the sand, talking to a boy of thirteen and a girl of ten; they have taken an immediate fancy to him.

Lenz

The last time I was at the beach was during the war.

The Girl

Did they fight on the beach?

The Boy

No, you silly.

Lenz

That beach was west of here — in Belgium. We were so glad to be there — we threw off our uniforms and ran into the sea like mad.

The Girl

With your guns?

Lenz (laughing)

No, we left them behind. But not far behind, because we'd hear the surf roar, and then every once in a while we'd hear something louder —

> (he looks off into the distance)

— that was the big cannon at the front.

CUT TO:

124   THE BEACH, LOOKING SHOREWARD —

> Pat and Bobby, arm in arm, coming down to the sea.

Pat

It looks very cold.

Bobby

It always does.
> (declaiming as he walks in)

But we'll never be cold —
> (unseen by Bobby, Pat scoops up a handful
> of water)

— as long as we're together — Ouch! Hey!
> As the water hits him, he jumps as if a hot wire
> had touched him.
>> DISSOLVE TO:

125   LONG SHOT OF THE INN. TWILIGHT —

> The faint sound of a motor which grows louder
> as we —
>> CUT TO:

126   A PLAQUE:

> "GASTHAUS BLAU-WEISS"
>> DISSOLVE TO:

127   "BLUE-WHITE INN"

> MEDIUM SHOT OF THE INN, showing a big
> Buick stopping in front. Out of it steps Breuer.
> He pauses to glance at the darkening beach, and
> then mounts the steps.
>> CUT TO:

128   THE RECEPTION HALL —

> — a clean, middle-class seaside inn, really a board-
> ing house. Victorian furniture, a porter's desk.

Fraulein Muller, the proprietress, a very old gentle-
woman, greets him. He clicks his heels and bows
in his most important manner.

Fraulein Muller

Good morning.

Breuer

My name is Breuer — have you a room for the night?
        She opens a register on the desk.

Fraulein Muller

Our season doesn't start till next week. We only have a few
people.

Breuer (signing and scanning the register)

I was expecting to meet some friends. Fraulein Hollmann —

Fraulein Muller

Three people came today, but they were in such a hurry
to go swimming they haven't registered. There was a single
man and a young couple.

Breuer (aghast)

What!

Fraulein Muller

I *took* them for a newly married couple and put their bags
in the same room.

Breuer (furious)

Impossible. Where are they now?

Fraulein Muller (pointing)

Out on the terrace.

DISSOLVE TO:

129   THE TERRACE OF THE INN — TWILIGHT —

— Pat, Bobby and Lenz have finished dinner. Empty coffee cups and glasses. Below the terrace, two strolling musicians with accordion and guitar, are singing "Freut euch des Lebens." *

Breuer comes out of the inn.

Pat (surprised and displeased)

Well, hello, Erich.
          (Breuer kisses her hand coolly)
You know Mr. Lenz and Mr. Lohkamp.
They rise and bow. Bobby not very cordially.

Breuer

I've had the pleasure. May I?
          (he sits down)

Pat

What are you doing here?

Breuer

I frequently come to the country by myself. It's a surprise to find you here.

Lenz

Have you had dinner?

* "Enjoy your Life," Nägeli (Hartmann, page 46).

Breuer

On the road, thank you.

Bobby (dryly, suspecting something)

Drive here in your Buick?

Breuer

Yes — did you come here in your — your —

Lenz

We didn't bring Heinrich. It wasn't fair to the rest of the traffic.

Breuer (not knowing his next step)

This is a fortunate accident.

Lenz

It was an accident that we first met.

Breuer

Oh yes, the race —
                    (looking at Bobby)
— and you won.

Bobby

Yes.

Breuer (carelessly)

It was a short distance.
                    (with meaning)
Over a longer course I would be quite likely to win.

Bobby (challengingly)

We can try it sometime.
>   Fraulein Muller brings a lamp, sets it on the table
>   and retires.

Breuer

You're staying in the hotel?

Lenz

We're up there somewhere. The end room.

Breuer (with a startled laugh)

Not all of you!
>   (as the music roars to a finale)
That awful music! Go away, you monkeys!
>   (he throws some change over the balcony
>   and the music stops)

Lenz (riding him)

Maybe there were two rooms — I didn't notice. What's the
difference — on the beach all day — just a place to dress
and sleep.

Breuer (with a double take)

Yes — what?
>   (then trying to smile as he asks Pat lightly)
You haven't gone and got married have you?

Lenz

>   (with the implication that Pat and Bobby
>   didn't worry about a small point like that)

No-o-o

                    (a pause)

Pat (suddenly)

Would you wretches mind it terribly if I went to bed? Remember, we've been up since six.

Breuer (disappointed)

Oh, I wanted to speak to you —
                    (stops himself)
— the next time I saw you —

Pat (interrupting him by getting up)

That'll be tomorrow. Goodnight, gentlemen.
                    (she goes into the inn)

Breuer

Just a minute, Pat.
                    (to the men)
You'll excuse me?

                                        CUT TO:

130   THE STAIRS — INSIDE — QUITE DARK —

                    Pat reaches the first landing. Breuer runs after her.

Breuer

Pat, I must see you alone. I've got something to say —

Pat

It'll have to keep till morning, Erich.
                    (almost pleading)
When I say I'm tired, I mean it.
                    She turns away.

CUT TO:

131   THE TERRACE —

Bobby frowning.

Bobby

So bad news has come.

Lenz (teasing)

Give him a chance — he likes Pat as well as you do.

Bobby (impatiently)

I'm going to bed.

Lenz

I'll keep an eye on the sea.
                        (As Bobby goes in, Lenz goes to the terrace
                        and calls over to the musicians)
Hey, boys! Don't go away.
                                            CUT TO:

132   BOBBY —

— hurrying up the stairs. He goes to Pat's door
and knocks.
                                            CUT TO:

133   BREUER'S DOOR —

— which is down the corridor and in half darkness,
slowly opening. The strolling musicians have begun
to play again outside — a soft, seductive tune.
                                            CUT TO:

134   PAT'S DOOR —

— opening. She takes a step out and is in Bobby's arms. We do not hear what they say but it is a long, passionate goodnight. Presently they break apart and he goes to his room.

CUT TO:

135   INT. BREUER'S BEDROOM. BREUER —

— closing his door and walking across to the window, frowning.

DISSOLVE TO:

136   INT. BREUER'S ROOM — NEXT MORNING

Breuer is taking off his pajama top when his glance falls out the window on the beach.

CUT TO:

137   WHAT HE SEES:
THE ABANDONED FREIGHTER — PAT

— sunning herself on a slanting deck. Bobby and Lenz are playing with a medicine ball on the sand. A little farther along are the two children.

CUT TO:

138   BREUER'S ROOM

Breuer reaches for his bathing trunks.

DISSOLVE TO:

139   THE BEACH — BREUER —

In silk bathrobe and beach shoes, approaching the hull cautiously so as not to be seen by Bobby and Lenz. He climbs up the low side of the freighter.

CUT TO:

140 PAT —

> Looking up expectantly; changes to a guarded expression as she sees who it is.

Breuer

Is this a private yacht or can I come aboard?

Pat

If you're going where we go. To very pleasant seas.

Breuer

Well — the company is good — at present. Pat, I want you to marry me. I'm really bowled over when I see you with these tramps.

Pat

They've had tough lives to live but they're not tramps.

Breuer (shrugging his shoulders)

I was in the war, too. That's the excuse for everything.

Pat

I won't even try to explain them, Erich.

Breuer (tartly)

No. Don't.
>   (persuasively)
I want you to come back with me today. I want you to marry me tonight. I want to give you everything you once had —

Pat (interrupting)

Please, please — I'm so happy now, Erich! For the first time

in my life. I don't believe it's going to last very long —
                    (very slowly and intensely)
— but while it does, I hate and fear anything that threatens
it.

> Bobby's face appears on the high side of the deck.

Bobby

Swim, Pat?
                    (he nods to Breuer and pulls himself up
                    on the boat, carrying an inflated innertube)
We have a life preserver.

Breuer (supercilious)

Doubtless from the garage.

Bobby (glances at Breuer then back at Pat)

Swim?

Pat (getting up)

Come on.
                    She starts up the deck toward the high side of the
                    boat. Breuer signs to Bobby to remain behind.
                    Bobby lingers impatiently.

Breuer

I want to talk to you a moment. I understand you've had
trouble renewing your license.

Bobby

You know that?

Breuer

A lot of things come to my attention.

Bobby

What has anybody got against us?

Breuer (shrugging his shoulders)

Who knows? Perhaps something political —
> We have seen Pat disappear over the high side of the deck. Now we

CUT TO:

141   PAT —

> Swinging by her hands from the edge of the deck. Only a yard away is a broken stanchion and if she could reach it, she could descend with ease, but her feet can't quite make it. A sea gull swirls near her.

CUT TO:

142   UP ON THE DECK

Breuer

I thought that, whatever the trouble is, I could perhaps make those in charge drop the matter.

Bobby

What are you driving at?

Breuer

I want you to let Pat alone.

Bobby

Oh, so that's it!

CUT TO:

143   PAT —

Struggling and panting. She has given up trying
to reach the stanchion and is merely trying to get
back up, for the drop is fifteen feet. She cries,
"Bobby!" but feebly.

CUT TO:

144   THE BEACH BESIDE THE CHILDREN'S TENT

Lenz looks up, sees her dangling, and starts for
her.

CUT TO:

145   THE DECK

Breuer

You claim to be Pat's friend. Well, look at yourself frankly.
What have you got to offer Pat? Do you expect her to sew
buttons on overalls?
                    (Bobby has no answer — simply looks at
                    Breuer in a dazed way, his thumb through
                    a hole in his bathing suit)
As if that would be enough for Pat.
                    (he shakes his head)
You're living in a dream, man.

CUT TO:

146   PAT —

Making a last violent struggle, an exhausting struggle. She gives a little cry, falls, lands on her hands
and knees in the sand. Then she gets up slowly
and begins to walk, gasping.

CUT TO:

147   LONG SHOT — LENZ —

Racing toward her in alarm.

CUT TO:

148   PAT —

Staggering, coughing, covering her mouth first with her hand, then with both arms, then falling to her knees, to her face amid the sea weed and wreckage.

Lenz (almost beside her)

Pat! Pat!

CUT TO:

149   THE DECK

Bobby and Breuer hear.

Breuer

Something's the matter.

He starts up the deck, Bobby following, still in a daze.

CUT TO:

150   UNDER THE SHADOW OF THE BOAT — MED. SHOT

Lenz is putting a towel under Pat's head. A dark stain is on the towel — Pat is on her back now, but her face is tilted away from the camera. The little boy has just run up.

Lenz (to the boy)

Go to the inn — get a doctor!

The boy starts off.

                                        CUT TO:

151   THE EDGE OF THE DECK — SHOOTING UP
        FROM BEACH

        Bobby and Breuer, looking down. Bobby, in wild
        alarm, swings himself over and drops.

                                        CUT TO:

152   BEACH

Lenz (shouting at Bobby)

Water — bring water! It's a hemorrhage!

        Bobby, aghast, gets his balance, looks around, finds
        a tin can and runs for the water.

                                        CUT TO:

153   THE PORCH OF THE BOARDING HOUSE

        The small boy, panting, meets Fraulein Muller on
        the porch.

The boy

Get the Doctor. The lady's bleeding — awful.

                                        CUT TO:

154   BOBBY AND LENZ

        — kneeling beside Pat — her face invisible, one
        fist clenched. Bobby pouring the cold water on her
        throat.

Bobby

Pat! Pat! Oh, God, we can't let her just lie here.

Lenz

You never move a bleeding soldier.
> (to Breuer who stands by, wearing an expression of horror, slowly changing to distaste)

Go get some ice.
> (Breuer starts off)

155   SHOOTING OVER PAT'S BODY TO BOBBY

— lying beside her, face to face.

Bobby

Oh, God, make it stop! Oh God, Pat.
> The little girl, on her knees, edges a little closer, staring wide-eyed.

DISSOLVE TO:

156   THE SAME SCENE TEN MINUTES LATER — MED. SHOT

(*Note:* I suggest an absolute avoidance of close shots of Pat. As we can't show the actual horror of the hemorrhage, it is best suggested from the distance of a bystander who cranes his neck to see.)

Lenz has borrowed the children's beach tent and is setting it up half over Pat to keep out the sun. Bobby still lies beside Pat, his hand holding her head. The Doctor, an old man, is closing his case. Fraulein Muller and a servant are setting down pails of ice. The children and Breuer stand near, and a dozen curious neighbors have gathered in the background. The Doctor gets up and walks aside to Lenz.

CUT TO:

157   TWO SHOT — DOCTOR AND LENZ

The Doctor

The sun may have brought it on — and getting off the wreck finished it.

Lenz

What now?

The Doctor

She keeps calling for Dr. Jaffé — that's Professor Felix Jaffé — I know him by reputation. If he could be brought here immediately —

Lenz

He will be! I'll phone to the city.

> He starts toward the inn. Turning back to Pat, the Doctor encounters Breuer. The latter's expression is even more full of distaste.

Breuer (nervously)

I never dreamed she was so ill. Will she die?

The Doctor (brusquely)

I can't say.

                                              CUT TO:

158   MEDIUM SHOT — WHERE PAT LIES

> Fraulein Muller, with a towel of cracked ice, gently moving Bobby away to set it in place.

> Bobby comes up to Breuer and the Doctor, his face wild with grief.

Bobby

Will it start again?

The Doctor

There may be other paroxysms.

Bobby

Isn't there something we can do?

The Doctor

Your friend is trying to get Dr. Jaffé.

Breuer (his interest in Pat has waned)

I'll help with any bills, of course. Unfortunately I have to
get back to the city this afternoon.
    (with revolting pleasantness)
Forget what I was saying to you — I know you'll be good
to Pat.
    (he nods, turns to the Doctor)
Spare no trouble, Doctor. No —
    (he catches Bobby's contemptuous eye,
    bows to the doctor and goes away.)
          CUT TO:

159   OFFICE OF THE INN
    Lenz at the phone.

Lenz (tensely)

— It's a hemorrhage, Otto. Get this now — find Dr. — Felix
— Jaffé. He's looked after her and knows the case. Tell him
to phone here. Somebody will be waiting. For God's sake,
hurry. Otto!
          CUT TO:

160   THE OFFICE OF THE REPAIR SHOP

Otto hanging up the phone. Jupp standing by.

Koster

Miss Hollmann's ill. Get out Heinrich right away. Great Snakes!

Jupp rushes out. Koster struggles into his coat and rushes out as we hear the roar of "Heinrich's" engine.

DISSOLVE TO:

161   THE HALL OF THE HOSPITAL —

Koster waiting. A nursing sister comes to him.

Sister

Dr. Jaffé is operating. Do you want to see another Doctor?

Koster

When will he be through?

Sister (hesitantly)

Well, he's resting at the moment — but he's about to start a pneumo-thorax —

Koster (interrupting)

Sister — he loves this patient — I know he does — and she's dying. I know he'd see me if he understood that.

Sister

Well —

Koster

Where is he?

> He takes her arm and hurries her off — she pulls him back just before he marches her into a clothes closet.

Sister (laughing)

It's this way.

> As they go out.

CUT TO:

162 OUTSIDE THE DOOR OF AN OPERATING ROOM —

> The Doctor, stretched on a folding chair, eyes closed. Two internes and a nurse nearby. Dr. Jaffé is a saturnine, bitter-looking old man with the air of hating the world and everyone in it.

> Koster and the nurse come in.

Koster (approaching him eagerly)

Do you know Patricia Hollmann?

Jaffé (starting — awake)

Never heard of her.

Koster (aghast)

Patricia Hollmann.

Jaffé

You mean that wretched little devil — that skinny little eye-rolling butterfly —

Koster (sternly and slowly)

Patricia Hollmann.

Jaffé

I know her. Don't look at me like that, young man. Where is she — in jail?

Koster

She's had a hemorrhage. They can't stop it.

Jaffé (springing up angrily)

And I'm supposed to break off operating to —
                    (he is flinging off his cap and gown)
I won't do it! I warned her to take care of herself. She was six months in a sanitarium last year. I told her she'd — where is she?

Koster

She's at —
                    (he hesitates, lies)
Not far from here. A little way out of the city.

                                        CUT TO:

163   THE BEACH — LATE AFTERNOON —

        Things have quieted down. Present are Pat, the local Doctor, Bobby, Lenz, Fraulein Muller and a trained nurse.

The Doctor (to Lenz after taking her pulse)

When will Dr. Jaffé be here?

Lenz

I don't know — two hours, perhaps.

The Doctor

Impossible. A hundred and fifty miles over mountain roads.
>   (he frowns)
The wind's getting colder — it's dangerous to leave her here
any longer. We'll have to take a chance and move her.
>   Bobby shrinks as the Doctor signals to two men
>   who stand by with a stretcher.

>   CUT TO:

164   "HEINRICH" with KOSTER AND JAFFÉ —

>   — speeding through the city traffic on two wheels
>   — down a one-way street.

>   DISSOLVE TO:

165   "HEINRICH" —

>   — tearing into the country.

Jaffé (above the engine's roar)

Very much longer?

Koster

Not very much.

Jaffé

How many miles?

Koster (casually)

One hundred and fifty.

Jaffé (a double-take)

Oh . . . What?

Koster

But only a few hours.

Jaffé

Stop it! We'll take a train. Why didn't you tell me, you fool?

Koster

You might not have come.

Jaffé

You kidnapper! You know that's a penitentiary offense. You wretched body snatcher . . . . Step on it!
　　　　　　　(they skid retchingly around a corner)
Is she your girl?

Koster

I wish she was.

Jaffé

A reckless, idiotic, self-centered child.

CUT TO:

166　　　　　　BEDROOM IN THE BLUE-WHITE INN

　　　　　Pat on the bed, gasping and choking. Bobby, the
　　　　　nurse, and the doctor beside her.

Bobby

Dr. Jaffé's coming, Pat. Any time now. Racing along the road
— nearer — nearer —

Pat

I knew it wouldn't last — it was too lovely — I'm sorry to be all this trouble.

Bobby

You should have told me.

Pat (with difficulty)

We shouldn't — ever — have met.
             (she begins to cough)

The Doctor (to Bobby)

She must not be excited.

                    THE SCENE DISSOLVES TO:

167   A MOUNTAIN ROAD

         "Heinrich" tearing along a winding course.

Jaffé

Where did you get this car?

Koster

I built it out of some other cars.

Jaffé

Will you build one for me?

             As they dash into a cloud of wind and rain, Jaffé
             lets go of his hat for an instant. The raging wind
             blows it off, to bound along the road. Without
             slowing up, Koster takes off his leather racing
             helmet and gives it to Jaffé, who looks at it as if
             it were going to bite him, as we —

DISSOLVE TO:

168   THE PORCH OF THE INN

Bobby standing tensely on the porch beside Fraulein Muller. Suddenly his face changes.

Bobby

I hear it — I hear it!

Fraulein Muller

I don't hear it.
          A purring is now audible.

Bobby

It's like an angel's wings.
          He rushes into the house and into —

169   PAT'S BEDROOM

Bobby

Doctor, they're coming! I can hear them!

The Doctor (looking at his watch)

It's impossible.

Bobby

There's only one car with that engine.
                    (he runs out)

170   THE PORCH OF THE INN.

Bobby reaches the porch just as "Heinrich" swings around the corner and comes to rest. As Koster and Jaffé step out, the country doctor comes out on the porch of the inn.

The Doctor

Professor Jaffé?
> (Jaffé nods)

Thank God you're here. We have so few cases like this down here.

Jaffé

Where is she?
> The Doctor leads the Professor into the cottage.

Bobby (to Koster with feeling)

Good work.

Koster

Now stop worrying. Got a cigarette?
> (Bobby gives him one)

How did it happen?

Bobby

Too much exercise — I should have known. If anything happens now —

Koster

Death's no stranger to us, old man. He tried to meet us at the front, didn't he? — but he never quite managed it. Now Jaffé's helping too. It's going to be all right.
> The nurse comes out on the steps.

Nurse (to Bobby)

Dr. Jaffé sent word to you that she's going to be all right.

She goes in. They look up at a lighted window
of the Inn where the shadows of the Doctors move
on the blind. Koster claps Bobby on the shoulder.
                                        FADE OUT.

FADE IN:

171   PAT'S BEDROOM. SUNNY AND CHEERFUL.

An old music-box is tinkling "Wann die Soldaten,"
and Pat is sitting up, dressed, in an easy chair.
She is thin and pale, but her face lights up when
Bobby comes in. He lays a bunch of anemones
in her lap.

Bobby

Roses, violets and lilies. How are you — very strong?

Pat (proudly)

This is the fourth day I've been up.

Bobby (sitting down)

Well, there's been some trouble.

Pat

What?

Bobby

Nothing serious — Fraulein Muller stubbed her toe.
                    (bending toward Pat)
Darling, you look —

Pat (laughing)

Only that?

Bobby

On that new bed?

Pat

What new bed?

Bobby (tantalizing her)

One of the guest beds she had to get so quickly. Darling, you look —

Pat (curious)

Guest bed? Why?

Bobby (carelessly)

Oh, for Lenz and Koster.

Pat (sitting up)

Have they come back?

Bobby

They insisted on being here today. Pat, dear —

Pat
(more and more curious)

Why?

Bobby

To see it happen, of course. You look —

Pat (wild with curiosity)

What happen?

Bobby

Our wedding.
> The music box becomes gayer as Lenz and Koster
> walk in, smiling.

Pat

What is this? Gottfried! Otto!
> (Lenz and Koster each kiss one of Pat's
> hands)
In the first place, if Bobby and I got married, Herr Breuer
would do you an injury.

Koster

No he won't, the twerp. Our license was renewed yesterday.
Breuer has withdrawn all opposition.

Pat

In the second place — I'm in no condition —

Lenz

No condition to be left alone. That's what we thought.
                    (the music-box stops)

Pat

In the third place, Dr. Jaffé said — that I might have to go
away —
                    (she falters)
— to the mountains — this Fall.

Bobby (with passion)

All the more reason to marry me now —
                    (their eyes meet with meaning)
— while it's still summer.
            Pat covers her eyes with her hand — then looks
            up smiling mistily. There are tears in Lenz's eyes
            as he winds the music-box noisily.

Koster

I'll get them.
                    (at the door)
All right, Fraulein.
            The music-box tinkles out a delicate waltz as if
            for the wedding of a marionette, as the Burger-
            meister, Fraulein Muller, two servants and the little
            boy and girl from the beach come into the room.
                                        FADE OUT.

172 FADE IN ON:
A SMALL YARD OR AREA-WAY —

— in back of a rundown brick house. Afternoon. An old-fashioned cellar door opens, and four men, one of them Lenz, come out cautiously into the yard and proceed toward a gate. As they open the gate, two shots ring out — one of them splinters the gatepost, another knocks off Lenz's hat. The men run — we follow Lenz over a high board fence, and then —

DISSOLVE TO:

173 BOBBY'S ROOM IN HIS BOARDING HOUSE

Koster and Jupp are engaged in putting into place some of the things from Pat's apartment. Matilda, from the garage, is cleaning. As the following scene takes place, they set down a couch, put attractive drapes on tables and bureaus and a fine coverlet on the bed, set up a white lounging chair, hang curtains that are already on rods, transforming — within a short time — a notably bare room into a pleasant and cheerful one.

Koster (setting down his edge of the couch and looking at his watch)

I wonder what's keeping Lenz. The newlyweds will be rolling in any minute.

Matilda

Such a difference the lady's furniture makes.

Koster (looking around)

Yes. It'll be nice here.

Lenz's Voice (from the doorway)

For a while, anyhow.
                    (THE CAMERA PANS TO HIM)
For a little while this room will be a little center of warmth
and light —
                    (he comes forward into the room)
— in a world of hopelessness and despair.

Koster

What's the matter with your hat?
                    Lenz removes it and regards the bullet hole.

Lenz

A peephole from here to eternity.
                    (he sails it out the door)
I oughtn't to bring ill omens here.
                    (he takes a bottle from his pocket)
Cognac from Alfons.

Koster

Who shot at you?

Lenz

Oh, I'm fair game. What's known as a dangerous man.

Jupp (at the window)

By Golly, they're here!
                    As he rushes toward the door —
                                        CUT TO:

174   THE OLD TAXI —
                    — drawing up at the door. Bobby helps out Pat

who has been reclining against a mass of pillows. Jupp rushes up, bows, smiles and begins taking out bags.

Bobby

Hello, Jupp. Now, darling, I'm going to carry you upstairs.
CUT TO:

175 BOBBY'S ROOM

Koster tying on an apron and putting the bottle on a tray. Lenz starting "Ubers Meer Grüess Ich Dich Heimatland" on the phonograph.

The door opens, and into the transformed room walks Bobby, carrying Pat in his arms. Koster starts forward clowning — but he can't, and suddenly they are all silent and very moved.

Pat (bravely and with vitality)

Hello — Comrades.

Koster (with feeling)

Welcome home.
FADE OUT.

176 FADE IN:
A TAXI STAND

Bobby, in the old taxi, pulls up at the end of the row, gets out, lights a cigarette. A big driver gets out of the taxi in front and approaches Bobby.

Taxi Man

Hey, fella, you better get out of here.

Bobby (innocently)

Why?

Taxi Man (truculent)

You ain't got no cap. We got too many guys already.
        Some other taxi men come up.

Bobby (pleasantly)

Friend, I haven't taken in five marks all day. That's why
I came here. I'll buy some drinks for an entrance fee.

Taxi Man (angrily)

We don't want no outsiders. Get going!

Another Driver

Ah, let him alone, Gustav.

Gustav (furious)

I'll count three. One —
        (Bobby sizes him up)

Bobby (stalling)

Wouldn't a whiskey taste good?

Gustav (unbuttoning his coat)

— two —

Bobby (losing his temper)

Oh, shut your fat face!
        Bobby slams him, connects; Gustav goes down and
        out.

The Other Driver (with admiration)

It won't hurt him. He's always asking for it.
               They put the man in the cab, and we
                              DISSOLVE TO:

177   THE INTERIOR OF A CAFE.
              BOBBY AND THREE DRIVERS AT TABLE

Bobby

I've been driving in the factory district.

The Friendly Driver

This is a good stand. More money than anywhere else in this rotten city. I'm an actor. Pete here is an architect.

Bobby (smiling)

I'm in distinguished company. Is there much work at night?

Architect

Sure — lots of drunks. A taxi-driver's best friend is a drunk.
               Gustav comes in, glowering.

Friendly Driver (to Bobby)

It's all right. Keep quiet.
               Gustav approaches menacingly; suddenly sits
               down. Bobby pushes a glass toward him.

Bobby (smiling)

Your drink.
               Gustav gulps it, calls the waiter.

Gustav (gruffly)

Same again all round.
>   (to Bobby)

Lucky punch.

Bobby

Cracked my thumb.

Gustav

Good.
>   The waiter appears.

Waiter

Two taxis at the hotel.
>   Two of the men get up and move out. The phone
>   rings again.

Gustav (raising his glass to Bobby)

Good luck, Maxey Schmelling.

Bobby (drinks — puts down his glass suddenly)

Excuse me — I forgot something.
>   (he goes into the phone booth)
>   CUT TO:

178   DR. JAFFÉ'S EXAMINATION ROOM

>   Pat sitting up on the table buttoning her waist —
>   Dr. Jaffé writing in a notebook as the phone rings.

Jaffé

I saw you four weeks ago.

Pat

That's right.
              Jaffé picks up the phone.

Jaffé (after a moment)

Yes, Pat's here now.
                                        CUT TO:

179   BOBBY IN THE CAFE BOOTH

              He hangs up, waves at Gustav and rushes out.
                                        DISSOLVE TO:

180   JAFFÉ'S OFFICE

              Jaffé and Bobby, standing in the foreground.
              Pat talking to the secretary by the far door and
              out of earshot.

Dr. Jaffé (gravely)

There has been no change. She must go to a sanitarium in
October. A year ago, she seemed so much better. Now —
              (he gestures pessimistically)

Bobby (slowly)

The world is full of healthy people who ought to be chloro-
formed. And this happens to her.

Jaffé

There's no answer to that one.
              (he puts his hand on Bobby's arm)
I ask your pardon for being able to do — nothing.
              (they turn toward the door)

Pat (grateful)

Goodbye, Dr. Jaffé.

Jaffé (affectionate)

Goodbye, my dear.
>Pat and Bobby leave the office. CAMERA TRUCKS in front of them down the corridor toward the elevator.

Bobby (unnaturally earnest)

You're getting better.

Pat (quickly)

Don't. I don't want to know anything — until Autumn.
>The elevator clangs open.

Elevator Boy (raucously)

Down!

DISSOLVE TO:

181   CLOSE SHOT — A CHESTNUT BRANCH

>It flutters in a sudden gust of wind — its leaves falling.

CUT TO:

182   A NEWSPAPER —

>— blowing along a pavement. ANGLE WIDENS TO SHOW:

183   A SHOPPING STREET —

>— on a cold Fall day. Show-windows with fur coats

on exaggerated mincing dummies of rich women.
Bobby and Pat strolling.

Bobby

If I were rich, I'd buy you a fur coat for Autumn.

Pat (smiling)

Which one?

Bobby (pointing)

That one.

Pat

You've got good taste. That's Canadian Mink.

Bobby (lightly)

Would you like it? I'll give it to you tomorrow.

Pat (without covetousness)

Do you know what it costs, darling?

Bobby

Money's no object. I'll sell my yacht.

Pat (alarmed)

Our friends would talk.

Bobby

Not another word — you'll have it tomorrow.

184   AT THE NEXT WINDOW — A HABERDASHER —

— exaggerated, comic dummy of a man in dress clothes. In the back of the window is a mechanical display — toy man and woman in evening dress on a circular track. They go in one door of a toy opera house and out the other.

Pat

You've got to have those tails to go with my coat.

Bobby (pulling her back to the first window)

But you're not dressed yourself yet. Two or three ball gowns.

Pat (pulling him to the man's window)

Shirts, cane, topper —

Bobby (enthusiastically)

Where's a jewelers? Where do they sell ship's tickets?

Pat

Egypt — South America.

Bobby (suddenly sobered)

There never was any South America.

Pat

I knew it. But darling —
>   (they are walking arm in arm in the
>   crowded street)
— it's all right here in our hearts. We can go to the most exciting place — home.
>   (they come to the taxi parked against the

curb. He opens the door and bows. Pat gets in the back seat)

Bobby

Where to, please?

Pat looks at him, shaking her head fondly from side to side. He nods understandingly, gets in and drives off.

DISSOLVE TO:

185 THEIR ROOM

Rain outside. Pat broiling a chop on a gas burner. Bobby on the couch.

Pat (looking out the window)

Winter's coming outside.

Bobby (his voice a little frightened)

No, not yet. You just think that because it's raining.

Pat (as if to herself)

It's raining. It's been raining too long. At night sometimes when I wake, I imagine we're quite buried under all the rain.

Thunder outside. The lights lower — brighten again.

Bobby (with feeling)

It seems to me we're lucky. When I think of life as it was before — I thank God. I never thought I would be so lucky.

Pat

It's lovely when you say that. Then I believe it, too. You must say it oftener.

Bobby

Don't I say it often enough?

Pat

No.

Bobby (melting)

From now on, I'll tell you every time I feel it. Even though it makes me feel absurd.
> A gust of rain against the window. A sudden knock at the door. Bobby answers it to find Frau Zalewska, the landlady.

Zalewska

The phone, Herr Lohkamp.
>   DISSOLVE TO:

186   DOWNSTAIRS. BOBBY AT THE PHONE.

Bobby
>   (repeating in amazement a question that has
>   been asked him)

"How did she stand the trip?" — What trip?
>   CUT TO:

186A   DR. JAFFÉ'S OFFICE. LATE AFTERNOON

Jaffé

The trip to the sanitarium.

Bobby's Voice (over phone)

Why, she's upstairs. I didn't know —

Dr. Jaffé (impatiently)

I told her a week ago she must leave. I told her this change of temperature could simply blow her away.

Bobby

She didn't tell me.

Dr. Jaffé

If you want to keep that girl of yours alive you take her off tomorrow — and I mean *tomorrow*.

Bobby

We'll go tomorrow.
                              (he hangs up in consternation)
                                        DISSOLVE TO:

187   THEIR ROOM UPSTAIRS

             Pat with her face in her hands. Bobby annoyed
             and tender.

188   FLASH OF CHOP —

             — smoking in the pan.

189   THEIR ROOM

Bobby

You should have told me, darling.

Pat

Oh, I couldn't. We've been so happy and it was such a little time. It didn't seem that a week or two could make any difference.

Bobby

We'll have other weeks later.
>   (she looks at him sad-eyed — Bobby resists
>   her firmly)

We'll get Frau Zalewska to help pack —
>   (to cheer her)

— and listen, Pat, we'll find Lenz and Koster and have a farewell dinner at Alfons'. We'll celebrate.

Pat

>   (half between tears and laughter)

I stole a week anyhow. They can't take that back. I stole a precious, lovely week —
>   (sing-song)

Pat stole a wee-eak.
>   (crowing)

Now you can put her in prison, but you can't get the week. She's got the loot buried deep in her heart.
>   DISSOLVE TO:

190   ALFONS' CAFE

>   A nine o'clock crowd. At a heaping table are Pat,
>   Koster and Bobby — a chair waits for Lenz who
>   has not arrived. Alfons, unusually magnificent in
>   collar, tie and coat, hovers over them.

Pat

It seems awful not to wait for Gottfried but it does look so good.

Koster (to Alfons, rather concerned)

Do you know where he is?

Alfons (glancing around cautiously)

I have an idea — there's a political meeting.

Koster (to Pat)

Anyhow I'll bring him to the train — if he hasn't got a couple of black eyes.

Pat (with feverish gaiety)

Alfons, I'm all a dither about how grand you look.

Alfons

In honor of a very fine lady.

Pat

But how can you throw people out dressed like that?

Alfons

Oh, can't I? I'm ready in two seconds.
>   (like lightning he whips off his coat — the
>   shirt front, tie and collar are in one piece
>   and come off with a click. He is ready for
>   action)

You see? — if they get tough, I do this — and this —
>   He picks a little man off a seat at the bar and goes
>   through the action of tossing him out the door.
>   Then setting the little man back on his stool, he
>   replaces his ceremonial front.

Pat

Alfons —

> (she pulls his face down to hers and rubs
> her cheek against him)

Alfons (retiring to the phonograph in embarrassment)

It is not done to kiss the maître d'hôtel.

Koster

In front of her husband, too.
> (he shakes his head)
I was afraid it wouldn't last.

Alfons starts the "Pilgrims' Chorus" from Tannhaüser.
                                        DISSOLVE TO:

191   THE SAME SCENE. AN HOUR LATER —

> — the food eaten. Pat at the bar having cognac with
> Alfons. Koster and Bobby at the table.

Bobby

We'll have to go home — our train goes at noon.

Koster (low voice)

I'm worried about Lenz. Somebody said there's street fighting
down in the Schmedgrasse Quarter. And he's always in front
of everything.

Bobby

You think we'd better go after him?

Koster

I think we ought to. I hate to drag you out tonight.

Bobby

That's all right.

Koster

You take Pat home and I'll be waiting for you in the street with Heinrich. No use frightening her.

Bobby

I won't tell her.

DISSOLVE TO:

192 THE BEDROOM IN THE BOARDING HOUSE

Pat's trunk and suitcases are in evidence. She is undressed, getting into bed.

Pat

I hope there won't be a bad dream.

Bobby (tenderly)

Let me come into your dreams.

Pat

You'd be very welcome there.

Bobby (hesitantly)

Pat, I've got a little taxi job — I'll have to go out for a while. A little more money for our trip.
                    (he bends over her)

Pat

I hate it when you drive all night.

Bobby (cheerfully)

But I remember you once said you didn't like people watching you when you're asleep.

Pat

I didn't. But now I get frightened that I won't come back.

Bobby

But one always does. I won't let you go away while you sleep. I'm an old wakeful soldier.
                    (he extinguishes all but the reading lamp
                    and goes out the door)
                              DISSOLVE TO:

193   THE MISTY STREET OUTSIDE

In the distance a roll of drums, distant shots, the scream of an ambulance. Bobby gets into "Heinrich" beside Koster and they roar away.

DISSOLVE TO:

194   ANOTHER STREET —

— crowded with truck-loads of police with straps, helmets, guns, gleaming in the lamplight. Young men in half uniforms are gathered in the doorways.

"Heinrich" drives through — stops. Bobby and Koster get out and walk to where a speaker is declaiming on an outdoor platform. In the general commotion we can only hear the speaker's voice as it rises to a climax.

Speaker

This cannot go on! This must be changed! (etc. etc.)
            the audience roars applause. Bobby and Koster jump up on a doorstep and scan the faces of the audience — lower middle-class and proletariat.

Koster

He isn't here — come on. There's another meeting down the street.

DISSOLVE TO:

195   EXT. THE FACADE OF A BIG GRIMY APART-MENT HOUSE

Small stores in front. Two trucks of police waiting. A small crowd listens to a yogi in a turban, preaching beneath a sign which reads:

"ASTROLOGY-PALMISTRY-FORTUNE TELLING
YOUR HOROSCOPE — 1 MARK"

CUT TO:

196   TWO SHOT OF BOBBY AND KOSTER

Bobby

What these people want isn't politics. They want a bogus religion.

Koster

Sure. They want to believe in something again — it doesn't matter what it is. Great Snakes! Look out!

CUT TO:

197   FULL SHOT OF THE STREET —

— along which comes a line of Sturmtruppen — simultaneously a bunch of young men and boys spring from the shadows and plunge a great plank into the door of the apartment house. A fight begins at the door. Some of those within resisting, some pouring out. Chair legs, beer glasses, etc., as weapons.

IN A MEDIUM SHOT, Lenz appears suddenly, grapples with a policeman. Koster grabs the policeman and in a minute, as the police whistles sound, the Comrades are safely out of the melee. They hide —

198   IN A DOORWAY —

— with a crying child, then they step forth and we truck in front of them as they walk down the street, side by side.

Koster (to Lenz)

I should think you'd have had enough. After four years of war —

CUT TO:

199   ACROSS THE STREET, FOUR YOUNG MEN —

— stop and regard the Comrades. One of them, wearing new yellow puttees, darts across the street toward them.

Yellow Leggings

There he is!

He fires two shots, turns and tears away, his companions with him, as we —

CUT TO:

200   GOTTFRIED LENZ —

— shot through the heart, falls dead on the sidewalk.

201   KOSTER AND BOBBY —

— kneel beside Lenz, rip open his coat and shirt. Seeing the wound they stiffen.

Koster (getting up)

Stay here — I'll get the car.
                    (he runs off)

Bobby (shaking Lenz)

Gottfried! Can you hear me?

Lenz's eyes are half shut, his face grey. Bobby listens for breathing, for heartbeats. Nothing.

Koster backs "Heinrich" up with a rush beside the
body. The street is silent, but there is a far-away
burst of machine-gun firing as they pick up the
body, lay it in the back seat of the car and cover
it with an overcoat. Koster and Bobby get up in
front and drive off hurriedly.

Lenz's hand, with one finger outstretched, pro-
trudes over the side of the car.

DISSOLVE TO:

202   EXT. FIRST AID STATION. NIGHT.

Bobby and Koster carrying Lenz's body inside.
CUT TO:

203   INT. FIRST AID STATION

A doctor in shirt sleeves showing them where to
lay the body.

Doctor

Over here.
(he pulls down a light close to the examination table)
What is it?

Koster

Revolver shot.
The doctor uses a swab, feels Lenz's pulse, listens
to his heart, straightens up.

Doctor

I can't do anything.

Koster

But the shot's over on the side. Maybe it's not so bad.

Doctor

There're two shots.
                    (they all bend over the body)
He died right away.
                    (the doctor takes a probing instrument from
                    the cabinet)
You can leave him here.
                    (he works over the body)

Koster (as if starting from sleep)

We're taking him with us.

Doctor

Not allowed. I've got to notify the police. We'll have to try
to find who did it. Here's one bullet.
                    (he hands it to Koster who looks at it stu-
                    pidly a moment)

Koster (slowly getting an idea)

I'll drive to the police station.

Doctor

I'll telephone.

Koster (stubbornly)

No. I'll go after them.
          FOLLOW Koster out the door.

                                              CUT TO:

204   EXT. THE STEPS OF THE FIRST AID STATION

Koster hesitates a minute — then his jaw sets and
he goes toward "Heinrich."

CUT TO:

205   INT. FIRST AID STATION — DOCTOR AND
BOBBY

Doctor

Can't you tell me how it happened?

Bobby (cautiously)

I don't know. Must have been a mistake for some one else.

Doctor (looking again at Lenz)

Was he in the war?
              (Bobby nods)
I thought so from the scars. He was wounded several times.

Bobby

Yes — four times.

Doctor

A rotten trick.
              (rather guardedly, guessing this is some-
              thing political)
And probably by some skunk who was in his cradle then.

CUT TO:

206   "HEINRICH" —

— pulling up at THE SCENE OF THE MURDER.
As Koster gets out, a shabby old woman is passing

— by the lamplight she sees the bloodstain on the pavement, starts and walks around it. Koster looks up and down the street — then at the bullet in his hand.

DISSOLVE TO:

207   CLOSEUP OF KOSTER'S FACE IN "HEINRICH"

— driving along a street, looking from left to right, stonily.

CUT TO:

208   INT. FIRST AID STATION

A policeman sitting at a table questioning Bobby. Another stands by.

First Policeman (moistening pencil stub)

Your friend's height?

Bobby

About —
                    (his voice falters)
Five feet ten.

Second Policeman

Can't you tell us roughly what the fellow who shot him looked like? Did he belong to any political party — wear any badge or uniform?

Bobby

I didn't see a badge, but I noticed he had on —

Koster's Voice (o. s.)

We couldn't see anything.
> (he comes in from the street)

It was too dark and it happened very quickly. There were the shots and then we only thought —
> (his eyes fall on Lenz's body)

— of our Comrade.

First Policeman

Do you yourself belong to any political party?

Koster

No.

First Policeman (suddenly looking hard at Bobby)

But *you* saw the man.

Bobby (on his guard now)

No. I saw nothing either.

Officer

Extraordinary.
> (he sighs cynically)

Then there's not much chance of finding him.
> (he bends over his statement)

Koster (indicating Lenz's body)

Can we take him with us?
> The policemen hesitate.

First Policeman (to Doctor)

Cause of death established all right?

Doctor (nodding)

I've written the certificate.

First Policeman (to Koster)

It's not legal —
> (he sees the expression of suffering in the faces of the two men)

— but if you want to, you can take him home. You understand that there may be a further examination tomorrow.

Koster

Yes.

Doctor (gruffly kind)

You can take the stretcher. Bring it back some time tomorrow.

Koster

Thanks.
> In silence Koster and Bobby put the body on the stretcher. One of the policemen scratches his head with his pencil — the other yawns sleepily. FOLLOW THE STRETCHER out to the street.

209   EXT. FIRST AID STATION

> Koster and Bobby put the stretcher in the back of "Heinrich" and cover the body with a coat. From the door, the Doctor watches.

210   TRAVELING SHOT — KOSTER AND BOBBY

> — very grim as they start off through the thin bitter snow.

Koster

We'll drive along the street just once more.
>   (Bobby takes a hammer out of a side pocket
>   and lays it beside him)

I have the feeling we're going to meet them any minute.
> They stop at a cafe on a corner. SHOOTING below
> its swinging door we see several pairs of legs but
> none in uniform. Koster opens the door cautiously,
> peers inside, shakes his head.
>
> DISSOLVE TO:

211 ANOTHER STREET — BOBBY AND KOSTER IN
"HEINRICH"

Koster (his eyes narrowing)

Look!
>   CUT TO WHAT HE SEES:

212 GROUP SHOT OF FOUR PEOPLE UP THE
STREET

> — seen dimly through the snow.
>
> CUT TO:

213 MEDIUM SHOT FROM BEHIND THE GROUP —

> — including the four silhouettes against
> "Heinrich's" approaching headlights.

> The headlights go out as the car coasts up and
> stops with a roar of brakes a few feet away.
>
> CUT TO:

214 KOSTER AND BOBBY —

> — getting grimly out of "Heinrich" and approaching

— to discover four harmless old people (comedy types) a little drunk. Koster and Bobby stop short.

The Old People (ad lib)

I thought he was after me purse! A girl's not safe in her own alley these days! The people you meet in the streets lately! Such wicked faces — scared me half silly!

Without answering, Koster and Bobby get into "Heinrich" and back away.

DISSOLVE TO:

215   "HEINRICH" —

— stopping at a sidewalk. By the light of a dim lamp one sees crossed flags over a doorway — a cardboard sign reads: "CLUB ROOM".

Bobby and Koster get out.

Koster

Stay by the car. I'll call if I need you.

He rings a bell, knocks at the door. It opens and he walks determinedly inside.

CUT TO:

216   BOBBY —

— lifting the overcoat from Lenz's face so that the snow falls on it. He watches tenderly.

CUT TO:

217   INT. CLUB BUILDING —

— a dark hall. Koster holding a sort of porter or non-com by the shoulders.

Porter (intimidated)

I haven't heard any talk about anything.

Koster

You're lying . . . . A man with yellow leggings.
            (he points to a door at left)
What's in there?

Porter

A club room.

Koster (pointing to the other side)

What's in there?

Porter

A pistol range. But there's been nobody here for an hour.
                                        CUT TO:

218   EXT. CLUB BUILDINGS

       Bobby standing beside "Heinrich." Lenz's stiffened
       finger seems to point toward the door of the build-
       ing as Koster comes out, shaking his head. Bobby
       covers Lenz's face again. They drive on.
                                        DISSOLVE TO:

219   KOSTER AND BOBBY IN "HEINRICH"

       It's just before dawn and they are drenched to the
       skin. The car comes to a discouraged stop on a
       narrow street just before it goes into a highway.

Koster

It's no use. They probably got off the streets.

> (he gets out, goes around and stares at Lenz,
> adjusting the coat a little as if he were still
> alive. He speaks as if to Lenz)

We've looked everywhere. We won't rest till it's all right.

Bobby (impatient to act)

Suppose we go to the police. They could at least help us find him.

Koster (fiercely)

We'll settle this ourselves. Do you think I'd let the police take care of it?

> (passionately)

If they found him, I'd swear it was the wrong man so I could get him afterwards.

> (a clock somewhere begins to strike five
> in a weird minor. Koster's voice becomes
> puzzled and bewildered)

He wasn't the sort of man you can spare, you know.

> There is a crack of thunder and —
> THE SCENE DISSOLVES TO:

220   A TRUCKING SHOT. THE SMOKEY REAR
AREA OF A BATTLEFIELD IN 1918.

Along a battered communication trench trudge the Three Comrades. Lenz is in the center, giving a helping arm to Koster, who wears a bloody bandage on a head-wound — and to Bobby, who has swallowed a mouthful of gas. Bobby gasps and holds his hand to his chest.

Lenz (in a hearty, cajoling voice)

Only a little way now.

(to Bobby)

Come on, son — you'll have a week in bed with pretty nurses chewing on your ear. Won't he, Lieutenant?

Bobby laughs and chokes. Koster stumbles.

Koster

I can't see for this cursed bandage.

Lenz

Nothing to see, Lieutenant — not a lady in sight. Does the Lieutenant think he's at the Kroll Garden?

(he sniffs)

No gas anyhow — Bobby swallowed it all. Keep moving — I want to get back and blow up the boys that got you.

With a burst of sound that might be gunfire or thunder —

THE SCENE DISSOLVES TO:

221   THE STREET. JUST BEFORE DAWN.

Bobby and Koster looking at each other across Lenz's body. The stiff finger points toward the highway, along which passes a procession of market carts — but now they are wintry looking and snow-covered. Two of the drivers are singing a melancholy soldier's song, "Argonnerwald."

Koster

It's morning.

(then remembering)

You and Pat are leaving at noon.

Bobby

Not now. I can't go with —

Koster (sternly)

You're taking Pat to the mountains this morning. When you get back we can settle this.

Bobby (passionately)

You swear you'll wait for me?

Koster (nods)

I'll wait. This is something we have together.

> They stand on either side of Lenz's body as the last market cart clops by and a pale wintry light breaks in the East.
>
> DISSOLVE TO:

222   A RAILROAD TRAIN —

> — leaving a grimy city station in the rain.
>
> DISSOLVE TO:

223   A THIRD-CLASS COMPARTMENT. EVENING.

> GROUP SHOT favoring Bobby and Pat who stand watching at the corridor door. Some passengers, notably Rita, a Spanish girl, are playing guitar, mandolin and accordion, and others are singing. Several, but not all of them, are thin and pale. Bobby's eyes are far away, expressionless — Pat is smiling.

Pat (to the performers)

Bravo, Rita. Hello, Boris.

Rita

Buenas Noches, Pat. (Good Night, Pat)

Boris (a Russian)

How do you do, Fraulein Hollmann?

Bobby (in a whisper to Pat)

You know these people?

Pat

Yes, from two years ago; they're going to the same sanitarium.
All the birds migrate about this time of year.

Bobby (considering)

Then it can't be so bad.
> As the music starts again they turn from the com-
> partment and look out the corridor window, elbows
> on the rail.

Bobby

In the Spring you'll be well enough to come back — all brown
with the sun?

Pat (without belief)

Yes.
> (a strained pause)

Bobby (making conversation)

Did you pack your silver dress?
> (Pat nods)
It's a beautiful dress — a dangerous dress. I hope it won't
make you unfaithful to me.

Pat (laughs sadly)

I love you too much.

Bobby (producing a little flask with a cup on it)

We deserve a drink. Pat, you've held up beautifully.

Pat

Not inside.

Bobby

That's why we'll have a drink.
                    (she drinks the cognac)
Good?
                    (Pat nods, leans against his shoulder)

Pat

Oh, darling, what is the good?

Bobby

Keep your chin up — I've been so proud of you all day.
                    (holds her close)
It's just the day you leave. Then things get all right again.

Pat

I haven't been brave. You didn't notice. That's all.

Bobby

That's just it. As long as you don't give in, you're bigger than what happens to you. Lenz taught me that.

Pat

Why did he miss the train?
                    (she doesn't know the truth but anything
                    is enough to accentuate her sadness)

Oh, Bobby, I'm afraid — afraid of the last great fear. You don't know what fear is.

Bobby

I certainly do.

Voice (off-scene)

Tickets, please.

> The conductor (a fat comedian) is having difficulty squeezing along the corridor. Bobby hands him the ticket.

Conductor

I've seen the lady's ticket already.

Bobby

Yes — in the sleeper.

Conductor

She must go up there. It's too crowded back here.

Voice (from the compartment — referring to the conductor's girth)

It is now.

> (laughter within)

Bobby (to the conductor)

She came to visit me.

Conductor (puffing, wedged in the doorway)

Can't go anywhere without a ticket.

A Voice (within the compartment)

That must be your trouble.
>   Bobby takes Pat's hand and starts down the jerky
>   corridor.
>   DISSOLVE TO:

₂₂₄   THE SLEEPER

>   They enter a compartment with lower and upper
>   both made up. Pat looks at a little slip stuck on
>   the door.

Pat (disappointed)

The upper is reserved from Frankfort.
>   Bobby shuts the door. She lies down in the berth.

Bobby (sitting beside her)

It's a good half hour to Frankfort.

Pat (doubtfully)

Well, there's that League for Fallen Girls.

Bobby

They don't have branches on trains.

Pat

Are you sure?

Bobby

Very sure.
>   (he bends toward her)
>   DISSOLVE TO:

225   THE SAME COMPARTMENT — MORNING

Pat and Helga Guttman, a plain, pleasant-faced girl, sit side by side. They have been chatting while outside the window snowy mountains glide by.

Helga

You were asleep when I came in.
    Bobby opens the door and enters.

Bobby

Good morning.

Pat (very bright)

Bobby!
        (indicating Helga)
Another old friend — Helga Guttman. She's going back too.

Bobby (bows)

Fraulein.
        (to Pat)
How did you sleep?

Pat

Fine. I'm all right now, Bobby. It's good to be going back — to be able to go back. There's tomorrow and next week and next month — why think any farther ahead than that?
        As she talks —

DISSOLVE TO:

226   A RAILROAD STATION IN THE MOUNTAINS

Sun, bright snow, a blue sky — happy, laughing people on the platform and the air of a winter resort. Two men in plus fours bear Helga away to a sleigh. Bobby is surprised by the contrast to what he expected.

Helga (waving)

So-long, Pat. See you at dinner.
Pat waves back. A porter approaches Bobby.

Porter

What hotel, please?

Bobby

Waldfrieden Sanitarium.

Porter

Waldfrieden Hotel? Will you go by mountain railroad or sleigh?

Bobby

Mountain railroad, eh, Pat?

DISSOLVE TO:

227   A MOUNTAIN RAILROAD OR FUNICULAR *

Pat, Bobby and others, including a nurse and a stretcher-patient, are seated in the car which begins to rise slowly up the mountain.

At the top, looking small as a pin-point, is the sanitarium — at the bottom, gradually receding, is the station and the little village.

---

* Built on a mountain side at an angle of 45° to 90°. There are two parallel tracks and two cars. These are connected by a cable which passes around a wheel at the top, and the two cars pull each other alternately up and down. These are all over Central Europe.

Bobby

What works it?

Pat

Another car takes on water at the top and pulls this one up. See it?

CUT TO:

228   LONG SHOT — THE OTHER CAR

— beginning its descent of the mountain.

CUT TO:

229   THE ASCENDING CAR

Bobby

Great idea. I wonder who thought of it. Is that the hotel?

CUT TO:

230   LONG SHOT OF THE SANITARIUM AT THE TOP

CUT TO:

231   THE ASCENDING CAR

Pat (looking up and nodding)

Hospitals look very beautiful — when you need them.

Bobby (looking down)

We're between two worlds. That's our train puffing away — it's hard to believe that I've got to go back to that world this afternoon.

Pat (alarmed)

Not right away — you'll stay a week.

Bobby (lightly)

Oh no. They'll put you to bed for a while.

Pat (pleading)

Two or three days anyhow.
              (excitedly)
Maybe they'll let me stay up.

Bobby (as to a beloved child)

You've got fever now.
              (he lays his hand on her cheek)

Pat

Your hand is so cool — leave it there. So cool . . . .
              A bare branch moves slowly through the car, click-
              ing against the seats. Pat reaches for it but it is
              gone.

Bobby (looking straight ahead)

Pat, I've got to tell you something now. Gottfried — left us
— the other night.

Pat

Left us?
              (pause)
You mean he's dead?
              (as she realizes)
Oh, my God!

Bobby

He was shot — instantly killed.

> They stare at each other for a moment. Then slowly her face turns up toward the nearing sanitarium and the white sky behind it.

Pat (in a whisper)

Gottfried!

DISSOLVE TO:

232 THE SAME CAR

> — descending now, with its seat reversed and the sanitarium receding against a dark sky. Bobby is the only passenger and his face is set and grim. The sound of half-roguish, half martial music begins again as we —

DISSOLVE TO:

233 A LARGE OPEN-AIR CAFE IN THE CITY

> Koster and Bobby at a table in a middle-class crowd.

234 IN THE STREET

> — a platoon is marching past the open-air cafe — half a dozen officers and non-coms with brutal bullying faces, and their followers — thin-shouldered, spectacled clerks; blank-faced country types; thin, pool-room youths and pimply boys in their early teens. The sinister aspect of the personnel is accentuated by the contrast between the tough, remorseless leaders and the sheep-like troops.

> THE CAMERA IS HELD ON THEM five or ten seconds to suggest rather than dwell on this.

CUT TO:

235   CLOSEUP — Koster

Koster

God help us if that represents the future.

CUT TO:

236   REVERSE ANGLE — BOBBY

His eyes narrow as he looks across the cafe and
gets up quickly. From several angles we show him
obstructed by tables or by people coming and
going.

This is INTERCUT with LONG SHOTS of another
table — a man, seen from behind only, rises and
fades into the crowd. Reaching that table to find
his quarry fled, Bobby stares about wildly; in a
moment, Koster joins him. The music has faded
into the distance.

Bobby

It was him — I'd know those leggings anywhere — but he's
gone.

Koster

There's no use — we've got to get his name first. We'll try
it Alfons' way.

DISSOLVE TO:

237   EXT. POLITICAL CLUBHOUSE

The same that Koster entered on the night of the
shooting.

DISSOLVE TO:

238   AN INDOOR PISTOL RANGE

Four young men in semi-uniform are shooting at a line of new board targets. They are: (1) a short, fat, muscular man; (2) a heavy, dark brutish man; (3) a mean-faced "killer" type; (4) a big, fussy moron whose spectacles give him a false air of intellect.

As the fourth man shoots, one of the targets turns sideways with the impact. TRUCK UP TO a grey-haired man in civilian clothes standing near the targets. His expression is covertly interested.

Grey-haired Man

Wait a minute — the target turned.
> A flick of his eye shows that he is doing something secretive as he goes to straighten the board.
>> CUT TO:

239   THE FOUR PISTOL-MEN

Talking and laughing together.
> CUT TO:

240   CLOSEUP OF A HAND

Scrawling an initial — "B", "H", "T", and "L" — on each bullet hole.
> DISSOLVE TO:

241   THE SAME HAND

Holding four twisted lead bullets in it, each with a tag tied to it. PULL BACK THE CAMERA to show the man with Alfons, Bobby and Koster at a table in Alfons' Cafe. Koster has another spent bullet in his palm.

Koster

This is the bullet that killed him.

Grey-haired Man

An expert can tell which one of these matches your bullet. Then you've got your man.

DISSOLVE TO:

242   EXT. THE POLITICAL CLUB — JUST AFTER SUNSET

The martial-roguish music begins again as the four men who were at pistol practice come out and start down the street.

CUT TO:

243   "HEINRICH"

Half a block behind them and on the other side of the street, getting in motion

CUT TO:

244   THE FOUR MEN

Turning a corner, reaching a cafe. The first man drops out.

The Others

Goodbye, Karl.

CUT TO:

245   "HEINRICH"

Coasting slowly along. Bobby and Koster are discernable in the front seat.

CUT TO:

246 THE THREE REMAINING MEN

Marching jauntily. They pass a couple of street women who make way for them admiringly.

The Women (ad lib)

Where to, big boys?
Plug 'em where it hurts!
One of the men makes an obscene crack in a low voice — the others laugh boisterously. We are now speculating as to which of the three is the murderer.
CUT TO:

247 CLOSE SHOT OF "HEINRICH"

Bobby and Koster watching intently.

Bobby (warningly)

No closer! Slow up! Slow up!
CUT TO:

248 LONG SHOT OF STREET AHEAD

The three men have stopped. They chat and look idly up and down — not noticing "Heinrich." The second man waves and goes into a house. The music has now ceased.

249 TWO SHOT OF THE LAST COUPLE

— CAMERA TRUCKING AHEAD OF THEM. The choice is now between the "Killer Type" and "Spectacles." The Killer feels his hip pocket. The other man cleans his ear sketchily with his little finger and looks at it. They do not talk.
CUT TO:

250   "HEINRICH" —

— moving along with only a faint ticking sound through the gathering dusk.

CUT TO:

251   A CORNER

The two men stop. They shake hands and part. We TRUCK AHEAD of the "Killer" type down the street, see him begin to whistle. *But it is not he*, for we —

CUT TO:

252   THE OTHER STREET

The face of "Spectacles" as he walks along, wearing a faint frown like a premonition. "Heinrich" is just behind him. From a window a radio gives a sudden squawk and the man turns his head as it begins to play "Crazy Rhythm."

CUT TO:

253   CLOSEUP OF BOBBY AND KOSTER IN "HEINRICH."

Bobby (grimly to himself)

All right, Mister.

Koster

All right, let's go. Let him fire first.

CUT TO:

254   CLOSEUP OF KOSTER'S FOOT

— going down on the accelerator.

CUT TO:

255   "SPECTACLES"

— walking. He reaches the open end of an alley just as —

256   "HEINRICH"—

— rushes up beside the curb.

257   "SPECTACLES"

— starts as Bobby and Koster get out. Then he turns and flees up the alley reaching for his gun.

258   KOSTER AND BOBBY —

Start down the dusky alley, each hugging a wall.
                                     CUT TO:

259   A TRASH BARREL AT THE DEAD END OF THE ALLEY —

From behind which come two crackling flashes.
                                     CUT TO:

260   KOSTER AND BOBBY —

Untouched, continuing on. Two more shots ring out. Then Koster raises his pistol slowly and fires.
                                     CUT TO:

261   THE MURDERER —

Crouched behind a barrel, dropping his pistol and clutching his shoulder. He tries to pick up the revolver with his other hand, but — Koster and Bobby bear down on him.

Koster (fiercely)

You killed Gottfried Lenz. Death and hate — that's what you and your kind are peddling through the nation — that's all you know, so here it is —

> The murderer leaps to his feet to dodge around the trash barrel. Koster's shots catch him in the heart and stomach, and, clutching himself, he dives head first into the trash barrel.

CUT TO:

262   THE STREET

A policeman approaching hurriedly.

263   THE ALLEY

Windows going up in the gathering darkness.

Voices (ad lib)

What's that?
Who's there?

CUT TO:

264   THE POLICEMAN —

At the mouth of the alley.

CUT TO:

265   THE MURDERER'S BODY

Half in the trash barrel, legs hanging out. The sound of a loud whistle.

FADE OUT:

FADE IN:

266   A CITY STREET ON A BLEAK WINTRY AFTER-NOON

Bobby's taxi rolling along.

DISSOLVE TO:

267-268   ANOTHER WINTRY STREET WITH THE TAXI — THEN ANOTHER.

DISSOLVE TO:

269   A TAXI STAND —

Bobby swings his arms against the cold, holds his hand up to a prospective customer who doesn't respond — gives up and drives off.

DISSOLVE TO:

270   THE COURT OF THE REPAIR SHOP —

— blear and desolate. No cars except "Heinrich" in the work shop. The taxi rides in, passing the gasoline pump, snow-covered as if it hadn't been used all day.

Bobby gets out at the office door and reads the meter.

CUT TO:

271   CLOSEUP OF THE METER —

— showing one-mark-fifty for the day.

CUT TO:

272   INT. THE OFFICE —

Koster, adding figures at the table, looks up as Bobby comes in the door, but seeing his gloomy face, asks no questions except —

Koster

Cold out?

Bobby (discarding muffler and old leather jacket)

Plenty. But nobody rides.

Koster (cheerful)

The Christmas rush ought to start about tomorrow.

Bobby

Maybe I'll get Santa Claus for a fare.
          Koster pushes a letter over to Bobby.

273   INSERT: PART OF A LETTER:

". . . found it advisable to put all our repair work
in the hands of several large jobbers, and so are
giving up our policy of shopping it around.

Very truly yours,
WIES AUTO-ACCIDENT INSURANCE
Per K.S.R."

274   INT. OFFICE OF REPAIR SHOP —

Bobby (in a hushed voice)

Will we have to go out of business?

Koster (rising and opening a wall locker)

Oh no. After Christmas there'll be jobs. Right now every-
body's trying to make the old bus last through the holidays.
               (a knock at the door. Koster, who has just
               taken out a bottle, puts it back hastily)
Come in.

(Matilda comes in. She is wrapped in
shawls, wears a Queen Mary hat and carries
a net bag)

Oh — Matilda!

(he takes out the bottle)

Matilda

Good evening, gentlemen.
Koster inverts the bottle over a glass.

Bobby (to Matilda)

Got another job?

Matilda

I have several jobs now, thank you, Herr Lohkamp.

(but her eyes are fixed on the more important matter of the bottle — which won't
pour)

Koster (rather dismally)

Well, that's that. And it's our last drop.

Matilda (taking off her bonnet)

My new gentleman orders his rum by the case.

(she opens her net bag)

He drinks far too much.

(she produces a bottle, takes out the cork
and sets it on the table)

But the very best.

Bobby (with feeling)

Matilda — I love you.

(he fills three glasses)

Matilda (haughty in her turn)

No customers' rum, that.
                    (they are really grateful)

Bobby and Koster (raising their glasses)

Pros't, Matilda.
                    (they drink)
          They look hungrily at the bottle again but Matilda
          corks it and puts it back in the handbag.

Matilda

It isn't proper to leave bottles about.
                    (she looks around the room)
This room! I declare, I'll sweep it out for you.
          She puts on an apron and goes to fetch a broom
          — during the beginning of the next scene she is
          in and about, always in the background. Bobby
          and Koster sit facing each other, smoking.

Bobby (dreamily)

A customer will ring up in half a minute — with a big job.
You'll see — half a minute.
          Koster takes out his watch. Silence, save for Ma-
          tilda moving about.

Bobby

Half a minute.

Koster

Twenty seconds to go . . . fifteen seconds —

Bobby

All right, you'll see.

Koster

Four seconds — three seconds — two seconds — one second —
(the phone rings loud and startling. They both spring up, looking at each other in awe. Bobby answers)

Bobby

What? . . . . Oh, hello — yes, yes — a job — yes.
(Koster gives a dance kick with excitement and turns to stare at Bobby)
. . . Yes, it sounds fine. What's the price?

Koster (in a stage whisper)

For the love of heaven, what is it?

Bobby

Shh!
(to the phone)
Oh, that's the price.

Koster (wildly)

Double it — double it!

Bobby (to Koster)

He says I only have to name the price.
(to the phone)
Would you consider doubling your offer?
(Koster comes toward him in agony, his hands outstretched)

Koster

Great Snakes! *Will* you tell me what it is?

Bobby waves him silent but he gives a wild yell and collapses on his back on the desk, his feet in the air.

Bobby

Now just repeat that — my partner is not very well.

CUT TO:

275 ALFONS' CAFE —

Alfons on the phone, smiling.

Alfons

You play piano for two hours for these cattlesellers and I'll give you five marks — ten marks — what you want, Bobby.

CUT TO:

276 THE OFFICE —

Bobby hangs up the phone.

Bobby

I'm playing piano for Alfons tonight. Ten marks.

Koster (letting out his breath and sitting up)

Oh-h-h-h!

Bobby

If they can stand it. I can. You see, Otto, there is a Santa Claus —

> (he breaks off at Koster's expression and follows his glance to the window. A pale face is pressed against the window pane)

Koster

Who's that?

> MOVE THE CAMERA UP to show it is the Jewish Driver who formerly owned the taxi-cab. He is poorer and thinner than before.

Koster

Oh, hello — come in.

> The face disappears. Bobby opens the door for him.

Koster (cheerful)

Come to buy back your taxi?

Driver (laughs)

I wish I could. I see you've still got it. How's it running?

Koster

Fine. What are you doing now — driving?

Driver (thoughtfully)

No, I'm not driving. I'm doing little jobs here and there. I haven't been able to get a regular job.

Koster

Tough times.

Driver (laughs deprecatingly)

There seems to be a little — prejudice around lately. But I must have struck the wrong people.

Koster

There're always some.

Driver (nodding)

Yes. Always some. You don't need any work done, do you?

Koster

We're looking for work ourselves.
> (the cupboard is still open. Koster sees a
> sweater hanging there)

Your clothes aren't very warm. Here — try this on.

Driver (grateful)

Thanks.
> (he admires it)

Not depriving you?

Koster (slowly)

No. It belonged to a friend of ours. He'd like you to have
it.

Driver

I'd be glad to tune up the Ford for nothing.

Bobby

It's tuned to the last pitch.
> The sweater has started them thinking of Lenz and,
> sensing their mood, the driver backs out, wearing
> it knotted around his neck.

Driver

I'm certainly obliged for the sweater.

Koster

Put it on.

Driver

No, I'll take it home.

> (Bobby follows him out the door. The Driver pauses affectionately beside the taxi)

Well-made car.

> (Bobby nods. Driver moves off, pauses, reminded of something by the falling snow)

I thought I had a job today — but the man wouldn't give it to me —

> (very quietly; understated)

— because it was Christmas.

> HOLD THE CAMERA ON his face a moment. Then he wanders away through the snow.
>
> DISSOLVE TO:

277   STREET OUTSIDE ALFONS' CAFE —

FLASH OF THE SEMI-UNIFORMED MEN marching thru the snow to the same mocking music. Far away an ambulance screams in the night.
DISSOLVE TO:

278   INT. ALFONS' CAFE —

Alfons is looking at the above scene through the window. He turns away with a frown. The cafe is crowded. A twelve-foot silver fir tree stands beside the bar, hung with colored balls, candles and tinsels. Two cafe women are putting on the finishing touches. In the rear, waiters set a big table — silver dishes over spirit lamps hold two suckling pigs with apples in their mouths and little fir sprigs ablaze upon their backs.

Bobby at the piano, is playing American jazz — "Among My Souvenirs," "Muddy Water," "Blue Room," "So Blue," etc. — and Koster is at a table surrounded by rough well-to-do cattlemen in cow-hide boots. The patrons are moving to the table to sit down.

Now Bobby stops playing, pauses and then leading a quartet beside the piano, begins "O du Frohliche, Ö du Selige." * Between the second and third verses a waiter comes up to Bobby.

Waiter

A phone call, Bobby.
> (Bobby nods, not really realizing what the man has said. After the number is finished the man comes back)

It's a long distance call for you.

Bobby (jumping up)

Why didn't you tell me?
> He dashes for the phone booth and another man sits down at the piano and plays, "I Can't Give You Anything but Love Baby," which continues quietly through the ensuing scene.

CUT TO:

279   THE PHONE BOOTH —

Bobby

Hello. Waldfrieden — yes —

CUT TO:

280   QUICK TRAVELING SHOT OF A LINE OF TELEPHONE POLES IN WINTER —

The line goes up a snowy mountain.

CUT TO:

* Teich, Weihnachts Album. Page 5.

281 PAT'S ROOM IN THE SANITARIUM —

— bare, white, cheerful. She lies on her bed, half dressed for a party, the silver dress beside her. She is thinner and paler than when we last saw her.

Pat

I tried to call you, dearest — I tried the boarding house and the shop —

Bobby (astonished)

My God, are you really there?

Pat

Yes. I'm lying on my bed in my room.

CUT TO:

282 THE PHONE BOOTH

Bobby (groans)

Ach, this wretched money! If I had any I'd be in an aeroplane in five minutes.

Pat (sadly)

Oh, darling —
            Pause — the wire hums.

Bobby

Are you still there, Pat?

CUT TO:

283   PAT'S BEDROOM

Pat

Yes, Bobby, but you mustn't say things like that. You make my nose tingle.

                                        CUT TO:

284   BOBBY IN THE PHONE BOOTH —

          — settling himself in the cramped space — head against the wall.

Bobby

Tell me everything you do up there.

                                        CUT TO:

285   PAT'S ROOM

Pat

Well, there're some dances this week.

Bobby

I'll bet you wear the silver dress.

Pat

Yes, Bobby — your silver dress.

Bobby

Who do you go to the dances with?

Pat

No one tonight. It's here in the sanitarium.
                    (pause)

This is the last one for me because I have a little operation next week —

CUT TO:

286   THE PHONE BOOTH

Bobby (terribly upset)

What is it? Why didn't I know? Is it that one where they cut the rib?

Pat

How did you know?

Bobby

Pat — I want to talk to the Doctor — right away. Don't cut me off — bob the receiver —

DISSOLVE TO:

287   OFFICE OF THE SANITARIUM

Dr. Plauten at telephone.

Dr. Plauten

She had a slight hemorrhage last week and she's run a fever ever since.

CUT TO:

288   THE PHONE BOOTH

Bobby

Is the operation dangerous?

Dr. Plauten

Not if she stays very still afterwards. It's a thoracoplasty — the only danger is a spontaneous collapse of the lung if she should move —

Bobby (interrupting)

I'm coming up. It may take me two days — don't do anything till I get there.

> (he hangs up and hurries from the booth, running into Koster)

She's worse. They're operating. I've got to go up there. My heavens, Otto, how can I raise some money?

> (Alfons joins them)

Alfons

They want more music, Bobby. I told them to be more generous with the piano player.

Bobby (distraught)

Yes, I'll play.

Alfons (noticing his agitation)

Rest if you want, Bobby. You've played an hour.

Bobby

I don't want to rest.

> He throws himself down at the piano and plays "Kitten on the Keys" or something very staccato.

289   KOSTER —

> — looking after Bobby and then silently going to the phone booth and closing the door.

CUT TO:

290 THE TABLE

Men are eating. Christmas stockings being passed
by the waiters, containing fruit, nuts, horns, etc.

A Street Woman

And here's the special one for Mr. Bobby. Because lots of
times he plays for us for nothing.

She takes it to the piano and hangs it from a song
album so that it dangles in front of Bobby whose
unseeing eyes stare at it while he plays.

CUT TO:

291 KOSTER IN THE PHONE BOOTH

Koster

Dr. Jaffé, you told me several times that you'd like to buy
my racing car. Well, it's for sale now.

CUT TO:

292 HALL OF DR. JAFFÉ'S HOUSE

The Doctor stands at the phone with a table napkin
in his hand. SHOOTING PAST HIM, we see his
family at dinner in the next room.

Jaffé (incredulous)

You mean that preposterous, ugly, rattling hybrid, that mon-
strosity, that four-legged road horror, that abominable jug-
gernaught?

Koster's Voice (discouraged)

Yes. I only thought —

Jaffé (heartily)

Of course I'll buy it. I'll drive it the rest of my life and then present it to the Transportation Museum.

Koster (relieved)

I'll give it to you in four days. But I need a little advance right now.

Jaffé

Come and get it.

CUT TO:

293   BOBBY —

            — playing jazz. Between numbers, the Street Woman is at his ear.

Woman (coyly)

Look at your present.

Bobby (not understanding)

Present?

                    (Koster comes to the other side of the piano)

Koster (to Bobby)

I've got the money.

Bobby (springing up)

Oh, thank God!

Woman (pointing)

In the stocking.

Bobby (getting control of himself)

Oh — excuse me.
> (he opens the stocking, pulls out pink socks,
> a flask of rum, a green tie, half a dozen
> handkerchiefs)

This is — this is — impossible.
> (he is very touched. They laugh and clap)

I don't know when I last got a Christmas present. I don't
even remember —
> (there are tears in his eyes — really the relief
> from strain)

— it must have been before the war. But I have nothing at
all for you.

Alfons (his arm about him)

Play for us. That's your present.
> Bobby turns to the piano and plays "Silent Night"
> very movingly. The voices join in with beautiful
> choral harmony as we —

DISSOLVE TO:

294-303   A MONTAGE SHOWING:

"HEINRICH" ON ITS WAY TO THE MOUN-
TAINS. THIS SHOULD INCLUDE: WINTER
ROADS; STREETS OF COUNTRY TOWNS
DOMINATED BY ANCIENT CASTLES; PINE
FORESTS AND MOUNTAIN LAKES; NIGHT
SCENES — FIXING A FLAT BY MOONLIGHT;
SNOW FALLING; FINALLY MOUNTAINS ON
ALL SIDES.

CUT TO:

304   TRUCKING SHOT OF KOSTER AND BOBBY IN
         "HEINRICH." A SPARKLING MORNING.

Koster (staring ahead triumphantly)

We'd never have made it without chains.
                              CUT TO WHAT HE SEES:

305   A LONG SHOT OF THE INN —

         — half a mile away.
                                        CUT TO:

306   LONG SHOT OF A MOUNTAIN ROAD —

         — "Heinrich" climbing. A horse-drawn sleigh is
         parked in the road ahead. "Heinrich" comes to a
         stop.
                                        CUT TO:

307   CLOSEUP OF PAT ALONE IN THE SLEIGH —

         — wrapped in robes and smiling.
                                        CUT TO:

308   MEDIUM SHOT. THE SLEIGH.

         Bobby and Koster running up to Pat and embracing
         her, robes and all, from both sides.

Koster

Great Snakes!

Bobby

We thought you'd be in bed.

Pat

I got your wire. I've been waiting in the road for an hour.

Bobby (to Koster with intensity)

Otto, I *love* Heinrich. I'm grateful to him. I didn't think I'd
ever desert him —
                    (quickly)
— but I'm getting in here.
              He dives in under the robes and comes up from
              below, holding Pat in his arms.

Pat

Are you staying? Tell me right away.

Bobby

Yes, I'm staying — until we go back together.
              As the sleigh turns Pat puts her hand into his chest
              under the shirt. She kisses him and tears roll down
              her cheeks.
                                        DISSOLVE TO:

309   EXT. OF THE SANITARIUM

              Large chalet style with modernistic touches. People
              going and coming with skiis, sleds, etc. Bobby helps
              Pat out of the sleigh as Koster parks "Heinrich."

Bobby (to Pat)

I can't get over everyone looking so gay.

Pat

Do you think it's unnatural?

Bobby

No, but I keep being surprised. How's your friend, Helga?

Pat (stops and faces him)

Helga's gone away.

Bobby

Gone away?

Pat (sadly)

Yes.

> Bobby understands.

> Koster joins them, smiling, and they walk into the sanitarium together.

310   INT. SANITARIUM LOBBY —

> — spacious and like a hotel save for the nurse at the receiving desk. Lounging chairs and sofas — card tables in use, a radio playing jazz, and a few people drinking what appear to be cocktails in the background. (Some of the types are normal, some thin and feverish but none very sick or emaciated — except when so specified in the script.)

> As Pat, Bobby and Koster come in, they run into the brisk young Doctor to whom Bobby talked on the phone.

Pat

Dr. Plauten — my husband.

Dr. Plauten (offering his hand)

Oh. I'm happy to see you again, Herr Lohkamp. Your wife is a great favorite with us here.

Pat

And Herr Koster.

Bobby

Is she behaving?

Dr. Plauten (lightly)

In a way. She is the leader of the younger set. Rather wild you know — cocktails, dancing —

Bobby (worried)

Cocktails!

Dr. Plauten

By the dozen.

Pat (ruefully)

But they're made of raspberry syrup.

Dr. Plauten (broodingly)

Cigarettes —

Pat

Without nicotine.

Dr. Plauten

Coffee —

Pat

Without caffeine.

Dr. Plauten

Dancing —

Pat (looking at Bobby)

Without you.

Bobby (shyly)

Is it all right for her to dance?

Dr. Plauten

It depends on the fever chart. Would you care to come into my office? I can tell you everything there.

> They walk off the scene. Pat's eyes follow Bobby lovingly. Without looking at Koster her arm seeks his.

Pat

Does he love me?

Koster (taking her hand)

He loves you, Pat.

Pat (still looking off)

Yes, he loves me — terribly. It will be very lonely for him.

Koster

That's silly talk.

> (they begin to walk in the direction of the bar)

What's this about an operation?

CUT TO:

311 THE DOCTOR'S OFFICE. BOBBY AND DR.
PLAUTEN.

Dr. Plauten

We take out a piece of the rib here — that's all. She lies
still for a few weeks — then she is up again and out — with
perhaps a new chance for life — a furlough that may last
a long time.

Bobby (terribly depressed)

Then she's sinking.

Dr. Plauten

The fever chart hasn't encouraged us. If she'd stayed in the
city things would be worse.

Bobby

But you only mean that it goes slower.
                    (shaking his head)
You haven't any hope.

Dr. Plauten

A Doctor always has hope. It belongs to his job. But — both
lungs are affected.
                    (Bobby shakes his head in silent discour-
                    agement)
Miracles do happen. Sometimes it stops, heals up — even
desperate cases.
                    (Bobby nods gloomily)
We have many patients about the same age. A legacy from
the war — undernourishment in the growing years.
                    As he talks there is a very faint sound of drums
                    in the room. Bobby springs to his feet.

Bobby (wildly)

Always that war!

CUT TO:

312   THE "BAR" IN THE LOBBY —

— where what sounded like drums has evolved into "Valencia" on the radio. Koster and Pat are sitting with drinks. Pat reaches around her own cocktail, takes up Koster's and smells it.

Pat

Yours is real — mine is what they call a "Special."

Koster (absorbed in his thoughts)

It's all been absolutely right, Pat. Even if things are as bad as you say, I'm glad you and Bobby have had this happiness together.

Pat

You're very fond of Bobby.

Koster (nods; speaks slowly)

Yes. It wasn't on the cards for me to marry and have children —
        (he drinks)
— and I've imagined sometimes he was my son — growing and developing.
        (sets down his glass)
But it was a pretty bleak world to grow up in till you came.

Pat (wistfully)

You think I'm what the doctor ordered for him?

Koster (nods)

You've given him everything he could have dreamed of.

Pat

It wasn't hard to give him everything.
> (nervously)

But now what do I do? I love him — so I want to know how to act — to leave it all clean and bright just as if I'd never been.
> (Pat should not lean too heavily on these lines)
> She smiles suddenly, and CAMERA PANS TO BOBBY, coming out of the Doctor's office. He sees Pat and Koster, bows to Dr. Plauten and goes toward them. They meet him near the desk.

Pat

Come and see my room.

Bobby

Otto and I have to get a place to live.
> (he turns to the motherly woman at the desk)

Can you put us up?

Nurse

Out in the lodge. Visitors can't stay in the hospital.

Bobby

I'll bet I can.
> (the nurse hands him a key which he doesn't take)

There's certainly a room next to my wife's.

Nurse

It's absolutely against regulations.

Bobby (to Koster and Pat)

You two go along.
>   (As they do, he turns back to the nurse)
You have a bee-ootiful face.
>   (smiling gravely and looking into her eyes)
>   DISSOLVE TO:

313   PAT'S ROOM

>   She and Koster stand in the open window. Bobby
>   comes in.

Pat

Success?

Bobby (dissimulating)

Absolutely against regulations.
>   (Pat's face falls)

Koster

We'll think of something.

Pat (sitting on the bed)

Tell me about home. Every day we can tell each other a
little of what happened while we were apart. Then we can
feel we've been together always.

Koster (feeling they want to be alone)

There's a rear spring in Heinrich that needs attention.

Pat

Good old Heinrich. What would we do without him? But
certainly you're not thinking about going back *yet?*

Koster (considering)

The little operation is day after tomorrow?

Pat (frowns — smiles)

That's another day. The important thing is the dance tonight.
If I haven't a temperature — I can go.

Koster

Then don't disturb her temperature, Bobby.
                    (he goes out)

Pat (arms around Bobby)

Oh, darling, darling!

Bobby

Ought you to go to the dance?

Pat

No. But I'm going anyhow.
                    (she looks at his serious face)
Bobby, all the time you weren't here I did everything they
told me. I was nothing but one long prescription. And it
hasn't helped. I've only got worse. So the time that I still
have — this time with you — let me do as I wish.
                    (her face is flushed and tender)

Bobby

I only thought we should ask the Doctor first.

Pat

We're asking nobody anything. *Nobody.*
>   (with an idea)
I know where you can borrow evening clothes.
>   (she pulls him out through the French win-
>   dows onto a little balcony)
>   CUT TO:

314   MED. SHOT EXT. OF SANITARIUM — BOBBY
        AND PAT ON HER BALCONY

>   — including another balcony below them and to
>   the left on which a handsome young Italian, Tony,
>   lies in a deck chair, wrapped in blankets.

Pat

Tony.
>   (Tony looks up, his face lighting)

Tony

Buon giorno, Pat.

Pat

You once told me you had two dinner coats. Can I wrap
up my husband in one tonight?
>   CUT TO:

315   CLOSEUP PAT AND BOBBY

Pat (whispering)

I suppose you've brought your own string?
>   (Bobby does a "double takem")
>   CUT TO:

316 MED. SHOT TO INCLUDE TONY ON HIS BAL-
CONY

Tony

Tutto quello che ho é tuo.

Pat (to Bobby)

He says anything he has is yours — isn't he cute? Also you're
being introduced — Signor Collazo, my husband.
(the two men smile and wave at each other)
CUT TO:

317 CLOSEUP OF TONY'S FACE

— full of adoration for Pat.
CUT TO:

318 CLOSEUP OF PAT AND BOBBY

— looking out from their balcony.
CUT TO WHAT THEY SEE:

319 THE VALLEY

— rather like Gstaad or Davos in Switzerland, with
sanitariums on the snowy peaks. Across from them
one road winds upward and disappears like a violet
ribbon between the hills.
CUT TO:

320 THE BALCONY

Pat (shading her eyes)

Is that the road home?

Bobby

Yes.

Pat

How far is it?

Bobby

About five hundred miles. In May you'll be starting back
along that road. Otto and I will come and get you.

Pat

In May. My God, in May!

FADE OUT.

FADE IN:
321   LOBBY OF THE SANITARIUM. EVENING

> Radio music. Men and girls in evening dress and
> heavy coats passing out through the doors into the
> night. General high spirits.

> Pat coming downstairs in the silver dress under
> a warm coat. Bobby and Koster in dinner coats,
> are waiting for her, overcoats over their arms.

Bobby (struck by her beauty)

Pat, you look —

> (he shakes his head, unable to express him-
> self. Pat nods understandingly)

Pat

You're rather like a Grand Duke yourself. And Otto — well,
that's service.

Koster

Ought to be — it's the head waiter's.

> They walk through the lobby, stopping to speak briefly to Tony and a party, and Rita the Spanish girl who is between two admirers — Boris the Russian, more emaciated than on the train, and Herr Heffrich, a Dutchman, who looks fat and well. They pass Dr. Plauten who frowns as he sees Pat — he starts to speak to her, hesitates, decides not to.

CUT TO:

322   EXT. THE STEPS ABOVE THE WAITING SLEIGHS

> The group pauses to look at the night scene below. Pat's face suddenly wears an abstracted look.

Bobby (noticing an unusual mood)

What is it? What are you listening for?

Pat (in a trance)

I don't know — I feel as if I were getting ready for something.

Koster (reassuringly)

You are — for the ball.

DISSOLVE TO:

323   A LONG SHOT OF THE KURSAL IN THE VALLEY BELOW

> Lights blazing, music drifting up faintly, sleighbells jingling.

DISSOLVE TO:

324 THE PARTY IN A SLEIGH —

— swinging along a white road between other sleighs — passing a sleigh with an exchange of gay cries.

DISSOLVE TO:

325 FULL SHOT — THE BALL ROOM AT THE KURSAL, OR CASINO

The orchestra is playing the "Blue Danube" and the guests are doing the old-fashioned "Wiener Waltz."

Pat has just finished dancing with Tony who bows and retires as Bobby takes over.

Bobby (with exaggerated carelessness as they start off)

That's a chap you might fall in love with. Don't you agree?

Pat (innocently)

Not exactly. But I don't know how I'd have done without him all the time you were gone.

Bobby

Haven't you ever been tempted here?

Pat

Not very much.

Bobby (torturing himself)

Hasn't it been hard to be faithful in that silver dress?

Pat (lightly)

On the contrary. It has memories, this dress.

Bobby (ruefully)

Yes, I know its effect. But whatever you've done, I don't want to know about it. It's all past and forgotten.

Pat

>   (undisturbed — whatever she's done, she
>   has no sense of guilt)

But I've done nothing.

>   (tenderly)

I love you too much.

DISSOLVE TO:

326   A CORNER OF THE KURSAL — LATER —

>   — with lights playing on the dancers. The orchestra
>   is playing "My Blue Heaven" in "sweet" time.*
>   Bobby and Pat are dancing a little apart from the
>   others.

CUT TO:

327   CLOSEUP OF PAT'S LIPS —

>   — saying something we cannot hear.

CUT TO:

328   REVERSE CLOSEUP OF BOBBY —

>   — showing his reaction to what she says. Implica-
>   tion of passion in both her whisper and his re-
>   sponse but no words in this scene.

DISSOLVE TO:

* This song is specified because of its nostalgic quality, desirable in this sequence.

329 THE GUESTS AT SUPPER AT LITTLE TABLES

MOVE CAMERA UP TO CORNER OF THE ROOM where Rita sits in the center, playing a guitar — something sad, Slavic and disturbing. At her feet sits Boris the Russian; behind the sofa stands Herr Heffrich the Dutchman. Both look at her adoringly.

At a table right next to this group sit Pat, Bobby and Koster. A girl in front coughs convulsively as the music dies away.

CUT TO:

330 THE GIRL —

— looking quickly into her handkerchief and flinching.

CUT TO:

331 GROUP SHOT FAVORING RITA, BORIS AND THE DUTCHMAN — INCLUDING PAT AND BOBBY

Boris sits up beside Rita on the sofa.

Boris (eagerly)

I can dance the next dance with you, Rita. I gained a pound this week.

Rita (sniffing)

Only one pound? Heffrich has gained four.
                    (to the Dutchman)
Haven't you, dear?

Heffrich (swelling with pride)

Not only that — my average afternoon temperature was only one hundred point-one.

> (Rita eyes him fondly as he turns to Boris)

And you're hovering around a hundred and two point-five every day.

Boris (heatedly)

That's a lie! He shakes the thermometer down. Everyone knows.

> (people begin to listen)

And I've seen your X-ray chart.

> (he makes a gesture of revulsion)

When you're out of the way, it'll be my turn.

> Over the back of the sofa they lunge at each other and in a moment the brawl is raging.

CUT TO:

332   PAT'S TABLE

Bobby (smiling)

Is that what you call love by degrees?

Pat (laughing)

Love by the pound. You don't know whether to laugh or cry.

> (looks at Bobby and whispers)

Be gay, darling. Be gay tonight for my sake. Who knows when I'll be able to go to a ball again.

> A fanfare of drums as we

DISSOLVE TO:

333 THE STAIRS OF THE SANITARIUM — MID-
NIGHT

Pat and Bobby walking up together. He has one
arm around her and carries her coat. Koster watches
them from the foot of the stairs.

334 CLOSE UP OF PAT

As she half turns to say goodnight to Koster.

Pat

It was a lovely dance. Goodnight, Otto.
Bobby and Pat continue to the landing and come
to Pat's door.

Bobby (rather shortly)
Now you go straight to bed. It's after midnight.
As Pat steps inside her room he stays in the hall
and starts to close her door.

Pat (in dismay)

Aren't you even going to kiss —
(he shuts the door on her)
CUT TO:

335 PAT'S ROOM

Pat inside the door, rebellious at this treatment.
CUT TO:

336 THE HALL

Bobby hurrying to the next room, unlocking the
door with a knowing look.

CUT TO:

337 PAT BEFORE THE MIRROR

— looking at a tear in her dress.

Pat (to herself in a whisper)

It doesn't matter. I'll never wear it again.
    She looks as if she were listening to something
    far off. Then she starts, and we see in the mirror
    that the door between the two rooms is opening
    and Bobby comes in.

Pat

Oh, Bobby! — where did you come from?

Bobby

My room — next door.

Pat (going toward him joyously)

Darling! Old times are here again.

DISSOLVE TO:

338 PAT'S ROOM SEVERAL HOURS LATER.

Pat and Bobby asleep in bed.

CUT TO:

339 CLOSEUP PAT'S FACE —

— showing that she's breathing with difficulty.

CUT TO:

340 TWO SHOT — PAT AND BOBBY

Bobby wakes, immediately concerned. Pat sits up
in bed, coughing.

Pat (in a rasping voice)

If I can only get through this hour — just this hour, Bobby — then I'll have one day more — it's now that they die.

Bobby

The operation's going to make a new woman of you.

Pat

That's Tony's radio there in the corner. Will you turn it on?
                    (Bobby goes to the radio)
Sometimes you can get an American station at this hour — it makes these times pass quicker.
            Bobby dials in. After a moment a voice comes on
            in Spanish.

Voice

Rio de Janeiro broadcasting — a programme of —

Pat (smiling wanly)

Oh, Bobby, do you remember — rolling down to Rio? — monkeys and coffee?
            Music starts on the radio: it is "My Blue Heaven."
            It continues through the following scene.

Pat

You ought not to have slept in this room. Not any more.

Bobby (unperturbed)

All right — then. You can sleep in mine.

Pat (dully)

And you oughtn't to kiss me.

Bobby (his arm around her)

I *will* kiss you.

Pat (leaning away gently)

No, you mustn't get sick. You have to live a long time. I want you to keep well and have children and a real wife.

Bobby

I don't want children or a wife, except you. You are my child and my wife.

Pat (dreaming)

I would like to have had a child of yours, Bobby. It must be nice to leave a little of yourself behind. And sometimes when the child would look at you, you'd remember me. And for a moment I'd be there.

Bobby

We'll have a child when you're well — a girl, and we'll call her Pat.

Pat (drinks from a glass of water)

Maybe it's better not. You've got to forget me. And if you do think of me, you must only think what good times we had — nothing more.
                (she sighs)
It's over — why — we'll never understand.
                (shakes her head; speaks almost imperson-
                ally)
I can't understand it — why two people should love as we do and yet one die.

Bobby (speaking with difficulty)

One or the other must die first. But we're a long way from that.

Pat

People should die when they're alone, or when they hate — not when they love.

Bobby (miserable)

We could make a better world, couldn't we, dearest?

Pat (nodding)

We wouldn't allow things like that. But what we've had couldn't have been better. Only too short.

DISSOLVE TO:

341-350   AN OPERATING ROOM

WE SEE A MONTAGE MADE UP OF THE FOL-LOWING FLASHES:

A DOCTOR'S TROUSERS AND NURSE'S SKIRT UNDER AN OPERATING TABLE — AN INSTRU-MENT TABLE WITH RUBBER GLOVED HANDS PICKING UP INSTRUMENTS — A NURSE'S HAND AND MASK AS SHE OPERATES AN ANESTHETIC MACHINE — UNDER THE OPERATING TABLE AS BEFORE, THIS TIME A CLOSEUP OF THE DOCTOR'S FEET, HEEL LIFTING SLOWLY OFF THE GROUND AS IN A GOLFER'S SWING TO INDICATE THAT HE IS NOW AT THE CULMINATION OF HIS EF-FORT.

A CORRIDOR OUTSIDE — TWO PAIRS OF
LEGS (BOBBY'S AND KOSTER'S) WALKING UP
AND DOWN TOGETHER — A CIGARETTE
DROPS, A FOOT CRUSHES IT, A HAND PICKS
UP THE BUTTS. THE FEET WALKING ONE
WAY. THE FEET WALKING THE OTHER WAY.

THE OPERATING ROOM, Nurses' and Doctor's
feet walking away from the table, instruments
being thrown into a steam boiler.

CUT TO:

THE TABLE — being wheeled back through the
building into an elevator, out again.

DISSOLVE TO:

351   INT. BOBBY'S ROOM

Bobby pacing. Koster coming in the door from the
hall.

Koster

Perfectly normal. Never was any danger and there won't be,
if she stays perfectly quiet.

Bobby

Can't I even see her?

Koster

Certainly. I've even got permission to say goodbye before
I start.

DISSOLVE TO:

352   PAT'S ROOM —

— darkened. The door to Bobby's room is open

and Bobby and Koster are standing beside Pat who lies in bed.

Koster (to Pat)

Don't you try to say goodbye — you save your strength for this husband of yours. Half an hour ago he was a lot sicker than you.

> (Pat presses his hand and smiles from one to the other)

Goodbye for a little while — Comrade.

> FOLLOW Bobby and Koster into the other room. They close the door behind them.
>
> > CUT TO:

353   A CURTAIN

> — blowing in at the window with a sudden draft.
> > CUT TO:

354   THE CONNECTING DOOR

> — which they had thought shut, blowing slowly open.
> > CUT TO:

355   PAT'S EYES

> — fixed on that door.
> > CUT TO:

356   INT. BOBBY'S ROOM

Bobby (firmly)

Otto, where are you getting the money for this?

Koster

Somewhere out of the future — it's nice not knowing exactly.
                    (he hands Bobby a roll of bills)
Why not draw on the future? We draw on the past. Why
there are stars still shining that blew up ten thousand years
ago —

Bobby (interrupting)

Where are you getting this money?

Koster

Why —

Bobby

Tell me!

Koster (hesitating, then very simply)

From Heinrich — it's Dr. Jaffé's Heinrich now. You see, he
admired him so much. . . .

                                                    CUT TO:

357   PAT'S ROOM

           Pat's eyes wide and staring. Pat's head shaking from
           side to side in dismay.

                                                    CUT TO:

358   BOBBY'S ROOM

           Bobby utterly sunk.

Bobby

That's worse than the money lenders.

Koster

I shouldn't have told you, you baby.

Bobby

This may be a matter of months, years.

CUT TO:

359   PAT'S ROOM

A nurse opening the door, looking at her, closing it. Pat's hand slowly comes out from under the covers.

CUT TO:

360   THE UPPER HALL

Bobby and Koster walking toward the head of the stairs.

CUT TO:

361   PAT'S ROOM

Pat's hand slowly taking off the bed clothes.

CUT TO:

362   THE LOBBY DOWNSTAIRS

A scattering of patients. Koster and Bobby pass through, meet Tony who shakes hands with Koster. Radio playing nervous music. "Heinrich" is visible through the front door.

CUT TO:

363   PAT ON THE SIDE OF HER BED

— slowly pulling herself erect, standing still a moment and then stretching out her closed fists quickly toward the ceiling and reaching toward death — the only thing that can save her love, her high honor.

CUT TO:

364   EXT. THE INN

"Heinrich" racing from the door with the cut-out open.

CUT TO:

365   PANNING SHOT — BOBBY

— rushing through the lobby again, brushing past several patients and running upstairs, two steps at a time.

CUT TO:

366   PAT'S ROOM

Pat collapsed in a heap beside the bed, dying. Bobby coming in the door — seeing — going to her —

Bobby

Pat — oh, Pat.

> (he raises her, supports her. Pat's head
> wobbles on her shoulders)

Help — somebody!

Pat (very low)

It's all right — it's hard to die — but I'm quite full of love — like a bee is full of honey when it comes back to the hive in the evening.

> On these words, before her eyes close in death, we —

FADE OUT.

367 FADE IN:
A SNOW-COVERED CEMETERY ON A HILL IN
THE CITY — EVENING

Bobby and Koster, their eyes straight before them,
are walking down a broad path. There is a faint
glow in the sky and far away the unmistakable
tp! tp! tp! tp! of a machine gun.

Koster

There's fighting in the city.
As they continue on, they are suddenly four instead
of two — the shadowy figures of Pat and Lenz,
grave and tender, walk beside them toward whatever lies ahead.

FADE OUT.

THE END

Notes

1. Even though Breuer does not go to the beach, I think
it is important that Bobby and Pat do not get married
until *after* her hemorrhage.

(a) To examine this: If the hemorrhage occurs *after* the
marriage, the implication is that Bobby has bought
a piece of damaged goods, that he has been "stung,"
and it lowers the tone of the whole romance, even
though it is not Pat's fault. In that case their sub-
sequent struggle is imposed on them by outside
circumstances and is not nearly as romantic as if
—

(b) He marries her on *his own insistence* in full knowledge of tragedy hanging over them. This is a challenge to the Gods, in full harmony with the romantic plane of the book.

2.   It may be necessary to cut the first trip to the sanitarium to a mere scene in which Bobby puts Pat on the train — so as not to break up the murder-revenge sequence by taking interest too far away. But I am not at all sure about this because the murder is pretty strong, so have tentatively left in the trip which runs six pages.

Appendix

KOSTER'S PARLOR TRICK IN SCENE 48

Floating Sugar

Effect

A lump of sugar is set carefully in a cup of coffee. The sugar remains floating on the surface until the magician commands it to sink — which it does.

Method

Carefully drop a lump into the coffee so the lump rests on end. Do this in advance. The standing lump is not seen. Use it as a support for the lump which you show the spectators. As the lower lump melts, command the "floating" lump to sink — which it naturally does as the prop gives way.

Afterword

Appendixes

Afterword

By Matthew J. Bruccoli

In July 1937 forty-one-year-old F. Scott Fitzgerald, having recovered from his "Crack-Up" but deeply in debt and unable to write commercial stories, went to Hollywood for the third time. During his ebullient years Fitzgerald had predicted that the movies had the potential to outstrip the novel, and he thought that he could always become a Hollywood success if he wanted to. In 1937 he went out for the money. His M.G.M. contract—$1,000 a week for six months with a renewal option of $1,250 for a year—made him one of the highest-salaried writers in Hollywood. Nonetheless, Fitzgerald was incapable of maintaining a take-the-money-and-run attitude; and he went to Hollywood with great expectations and strong resolutions. Writing to his daughter, Scottie, en route to California he explained:

I feel a certain excitement. The third Hollywood venture. Two failures behind me though one no fault of mine. The first one was just ten years ago.[1] At that time I had been generally acknowledged for several years as the top American writer both seriously and, as far as prices went, popularly. I had been loafing for six months for the first time in my life and was confidant to the point of conciet. Hollywood made a big fuss over us and the ladies all looked very beautiful to a man of thirty. I honestly believed that *with no effort on my part* I was a sort of magician with words—an odd delusion on my part when I had worked so desperately hard to develop a hard, colorful prose style.

Total result—a great time + no work. I was to be paid only a small amount unless they made my picture—they didn't.

The second time I went was five years ago.[2] Life had gotten in some hard socks and while all was serene on top, with your mother apparently recovered in Montgomery, I was jittery underneath and beginning to drink more than I ought to. Far from approaching it too confidently I was far too humble. I ran afoul of a bastard named de Sano, since a suicide, and let myself be gyped out of command. I wrote the picture + he changed as I wrote. I tried to get at Thalberg but was erroneously warned against it as "bad taste." Result—a bad script. I left with the money, for this was a contract for weekly payments, but disillusioned and disgusted, vowing never to go back, tho they said it wasn't my fault + asked me to stay. I wanted to get east when the contract expired to see how your mother was. This was later interpreted as "running out on them" + held against me.

(The train has left El Paso since I began this letter—hence the writing—Rocky Mountain writing.)

I want to profit by these two experiences—I must be very tactful but keep my hand on the wheel from the start—find out the key man among the bosses + the most malleable among the collaborators—then fight the rest tooth + nail until, in fact or in effect, I'm alone on the picture. That's the only way I can do my best work. Given a break I can make them double this contract in less than two years.[3]

Fitzgerald correctly anticipated that his major problem would be with the collaborative system under which movies were made. He did not work well with collaborators and, moreover, had contempt for the writers he was teamed with. After a dialogue polish job on *A Yank at Oxford,* Fitzgerald was given the choice assignment to write the screenplay for Erich Maria Remarque's novel about post-war Germany, *Three Comrades* (1937), under producer Joseph Mankiewicz. It was a major production, starring Margaret Sullavan, Robert Taylor, Franchot Tone, and Robert Young. M.G.M. was a "producer's lot," and Mankiewicz was a member of the palace guard. He had started as a screenwriter, and his writing credits included *Skippy, Manhattan Melodrama,* and *Our Daily Bread.* In 1936 he became a producer at M.G.M. and was responsible for *The Three Godfathers, Fury, The Gorgeous Hussy, Love on the Run, The Bride Wore Red, Double Wedding,* and *Mannequin.* The director of *Three Comrades,* veteran Frank Borzage—who had directed *Seventh Heaven, A Farewell to Arms,* and *History Is Made at Night*—apparently had no control over the script.

Fitzgerald submitted his screenplay on 1 September 1937: this was the screenplay published here. It is a competent job, but too long and rather slowly paced. (The production script was more than forty pages shorter.) Fitzgerald's problem as a screenwriter was that he was by nature and training a story-teller, accustomed to providing the reader with the kinds of information that could not be dramatized. One of the reasons why Fitzgerald's novels have failed as movies is that his technique was novelistic rather than dramatic, and no screenwriter thus far has been able to translate Fitzgerald's narrative voice into visual images. The opening of this screenplay shows Fitzgerald-the-novelist trying to establish too much background: the defeat of Germany, Pat as an undernourished child, the German inflation, and even an encounter between thirteen-year-old Pat and the three comrades. What might be called the Fitzgerald touch comes at sequences 54–55 and 57 where the switchboard is operated by an angel and a satyr when Bobby (Erich) makes his first call to Pat. This fanciful bit permanently disappeared in the first revise. After turning in his screenplay, Fitzgerald was worried that he would be stuck with a collaborator, and wrote Mankiewicz on 4 September 1937:

Dear Joe:

This letter is only valid in case you like the script very much. In that case, I feel I can ask you to let me try to make what cuts and rearrangements you think necessary, by myself. You know how when a new writer comes on a repair job he begins by cutting out an early scene, not realizing that he is taking the heart out of six later scenes which turn upon it. Two of these scenes can't be cut so new weak scenes are written to bolster them up, and the whole tragic business of collaboration has begun—like a child's drawing made "perfect" by a million erasures.

If a time comes when I'm no longer useful, I will understand, but I hope that this work will be good enough to earn me the right to a first revise to correct such faults as you may find. Then perhaps I can make it so strong that you won't want any more cooks.

Yours,

P.S. My address will be, Highlands Hospital, Ashville, N.C., where my wife is a patient. I will bring back most of the last act with me.[4]

Mankiewicz wired reassuringly on 9 September that the part of the script Fitzgerald submitted is "simply swell"; Fitzgerald should not worry about being stuck with another writer. This joshing telegram urges Fitzgerald not to believe the stories about illiterate movie producers: Mankiewicz knows that Shakespeare is under contract to British Gaumont Studios and that "impossible" is one word. Mankiewicz's wire ends with an expression of his hopes for the rest of the screenplay and asks Fitzgerald to return to Hollywood as soon as possible. [5]

When Fitzgerald returned, E. E. Paramore was assigned as his collaborator on *Three Comrades* to help with construction. Paramore was an experienced Hollywood writer who had worked on *The Thundering Herd, The Bitter Tea of General Yen, Baby Take a Bow, The Three Godfathers,* and *The Farmer Takes a Wife.* He was best known for his parody of Robert W. Service, "The Ballad of Yukon Jake," which became a standard recitation piece after it appeared in *Vanity Fair* in 1921. Fitzgerald and Ted Paramore were old acquaintances—if not old friends—having known each other in New York in the early twenties. In *The Beautiful and Damned* Fitzgerald had named a foolish character Fred E. Paramore. The collaboration quickly soured as Fitzgerald and Paramore disagreed about the latter's role in the project. Fitzgerald intended to retain final control over the screenplay and regarded Paramore as a junior partner. On 24 October Fitzgerald wrote Paramore stipulating the basis of their collaboration:

Dear Ted:

I'd intended to go into this Friday but time was too short. Also, hating controversy, I've decided after all to write it. At all events it must be discussed now.

First let me say that in the main I agree with your present angle, as opposed to your first "war" angle on the script, and I think you have cleared up a lot in the short time we've been working. Also I know we can work together even if we occasionally hurl about charges of pedantry and prudery.

But on the other hand I totally disagree with you as to the terms of our collaboration. We got off to a bad start and I think you are under certain misapprehensions founded more on my state of mind and body last Friday than upon the real situation.* My script is in a general way approved of. There was not any question of taking it out of my hands—as in the case of Sheriff. The question was who I wanted to work with me on it and for how long. *That was the entire question* and it is not materially changed because I was temporarily off my balance.

At what point you decided you wanted to take the whole course of things in hand—whether because of that day or because when you read my script you liked it much less than did Joe or the people in his office—where that point was I don't know. But it was apparent Saturday that you had and it is with my faculties quite clear and alert that I tell you I *prefer to keep* the responsibility for the script as a whole.

For a case in point: such matters as to whether to include the scene with Bruer in Pat's room, or the one about the whores in Bobby's apartment, or this bit of Ferdinand Grau's dialogue or that, or whether the car is called Heinrich or Ludwig, are not matters I will argue with you before Joe. I will yield points by the dozen but in the case of such matters, Joe's knowledge that they were in the book and that I did or did not choose to use them are tantamount to his acceptance of my taste. That there are a dozen

* Fitzgerald's trips east triggered drinking bouts, and he may have been recovering from a bender when he met with Paramore.

ways of treating it all, or of selecting material, is a commonplace but I have done my exploring and made my choices according to my canons of taste. Joe's caution to you was not to spoil the Fitzgerald quality of the *script*. He did not merely say to let the good scenes alone—he meant that the *quality* of the script in its entirety pleased him (save the treatment of Köster). I feel that the quality was obtained in certain ways, that the scene of Pat in Bruer's room, for instance, has a value in suddenly and surprisingly leading the audience into a glimpse of Pat's world, a tail hanging right out of our circle of protagonists, if you will. I will make it less heavy but I can't and shouldn't be asked to defend it beyond that, nor is it your function to attack it before Joe unless a doubt is already in his mind. About the whores, again it is a feeling but, in spite of your current underestimation of my abilities, I think you would be overstepping your functions if you make a conference-room point of such a matter.

Point after point has become a matter you are going to "take to Joe," more inessential details than I bothered him with in two months. What I want to take to Joe is simply this—the assurance that we can finish the script in three weeks more—you've had a full week to find your way around it—and the assurance that we are in agreement on the main points.

I'm not satisfied with the opening and can't believe now that Joe cared whether the airplane was blown up at the beginning or end of the scene, or even liked it very much—but except for that I think we do agree on the main line even to the sequences.

But, Ted, when you blandly informed me yesterday that you were going to write the whole thing over yourself, kindly including my best scenes, I knew we'd have to have this out. Whether the picture is in production in January or May there is no reason on God's earth why we can't finish this script in three to four weeks if we divide up the scenes and get together on the piecing together and technical revision. If you were called on this job in the capacity of complete rewriter then I'm getting deaf. I want to reconceive and rewrite my share of the weak scenes and I want your help but I am not going to spend hours of time and talent arguing with you as to whether I've chosen the best or second best speech of Lenz's to adorn the dressing-up scene. I am not referring to key speeches which are discussable but the idea of sitting by while you dredge through the book again as if it were Shakespeare—well, I didn't write four out of four best sellers or a hundred and fifty top-price short stories out of the mind of a temperamental child without taste or judgment.

This letter is sharp but a discussion might become more heated and less logical. Your job is to help me, not hinder me. Perhaps you'd let me know before we see Joe whether it is possible for us to get together on this.

This letter is an argument against arguments and certainly mustn't lead to one. Like you, I want to work.[6]

Fitzgerald could never accept the Hollywood condition that, having been hired because of his talent, his work would be altered by lesser writers. Around this time Fitzgerald wrote this parable about the nature of artistic creativity.

A FABLE FOR TED PARAMORE
(Then whom there is no one to whom it is less necessary)
by
F. Scott Fitzgerald

A great city set in a valley, desired a cathedral. They sent for an eminent architect who designed one distinguished by a great central tower. No sooner was it begun, however, than critics arose who objected to the tower calling it useless, ornamental, illogical, and what not—destroyed his plan and commissioning another architect to build a cathedral of great blocks and masses. It was very beautiful and Grecian in its purity but no one ever loved the cathedral of that city as they did those of Rome and Sienna and the great Duomo of Florence.

After thirty years wondering why, the citizens dug up the plans of the first architect (since grown famous) and built from it. From the first Mass the cathedral seized the imagination of the multitude and fools said it was because the tower pointed heavenward, etc., but one young realist decided to dig up the artist, now an old man, and ask him why.

The artist was too old to remember, he said—and he added "I doubt if I ever knew. But I knew I was right."

"How did you know if you don't know your reasons?"

"Because I felt good that day," answered the architect, "and if I feel good I have a reason for what I do even if I don't know the reason." So the realist went away unanswered.

On that same day a young boy going to Mass with his mother quickened his step as he crossed the cathedral square.

"Oh I like our new cathedral so much better than the old," he said.

"But the academy thinks it's not nearly so beautiful."

"But it's because of the mountains," said the little boy. "Before we had the tower I could see the mountains and they made everything seem little when you went inside the Church. Now you can't see the mountains so God inside is more important."

That was what the architect had envisioned without thinking when he accidentally raised his forfinger against the sky fifty years before.[7]

The first surviving Fitzgerald/Paramore revision was submitted in 5 November 1937; successive revises were dated 7 December, 13 December, 21 December, and 21 January 1938. The last script was tagged:

> FROM:
> F. S. Fitzgerald
> E. E. Paramore
> Script okayed by
> Joseph Mankiewicz
> 2/1/38

Although he did not get screen credit, Mankiewicz functioned as the third collaborator and performed an independent rewrite on the final script. Fitzgerald and Paramore received joint screen credit for *Three Comrades*. In his own copy of the final script Fitzgerald crossed out "okayed" and wrote "scrawled over." On the first page he noted: "37 pages mine about ⅓, but all shadows + rythm removed." At sequence 89—Erich's return to Alfons' bar after his opera date with

Pat—Fitzgerald wrote: "This is 'authors talking' about a script—This isn't writing This is Joe Manowizf. So slick—so cheap." And on p. 62—the scene in which Koster urges Pat to marry Erich—Fitzgerald noted: "From here on 17 pps fairly mine *not* Remarque or anyone else." [8]

During the reworking of *Three Comrades* M.G.M. picked up Fitzgerald's option for a year at $1,250 per week. Fitzgerald probably felt confident after he passed this test, and he began feuding with Mankiewicz over the producer's rewriting of the screenplay. Mankiewicz was a successful screenwriter, as well as the producer, and felt that he was equipped to improve Fitzgerald's work. In 1967 Mankiewicz commented: "I personally have been attacked as if I had spat on the flag because it happened once that I rewrote some dialogue by F. Scott Fitzgerald. But it needed it! The actors, among them Margaret Sullavan, absolutely could not read the lines. It was very literary dialogue, novelistic dialogue that lacked all the qualities required for screen dialogue. The latter must be 'spoken.' Scott Fitzgerald really wrote very bad spoken dialogue." [9] In addition to his pre-production revisions, Mankiewicz rewrote dialogue during shooting.

Given the layers of revision by Fitzgerald, Paramore, and Mankiewicz, it is impossible to be sure which lines and scenes Mankiewicz was responsible for. Fitzgerald's 20 January 1938 letter of protest to Mankiewicz is keyed to the penultimate 21 January screenplay.

Dear Joe:

Well, I read the last part and I feel like a good many writers must have felt in the past. I gave you a drawing and you simply took a box of chalk and touched it up. Pat has now become a sentimental girl from Brooklyn, and I guess all these years I've been kidding myself about being a good writer.

Most of the movement is gone—action that was unexpected and diverting is slowed down to a key that will disturb nobody—and now they can focus directly on Pat's death, squirming slightly as they wait for the other picture on the program.

To say I'm disillusioned is putting it mildly. For nineteen years, with two years out for sickness, I've written best-selling entertainment, and my dialogue is supposedly right up at the top. But I learn from the script that you've suddenly decided that it isn't good dialogue and you can take a few hours off and do much better.

I think you now have a flop on your hands—as thoroughly naive as *The Bride Wore Red* but utterly inexcusable because this time you *had* something and you have arbitrarily and carelessly torn it to pieces. To take out the manicurist and the balcony scene and then have space to put in that utter drool out of *True Romances* which Pat gets off on page 116 makes me think we don't talk the same language. God and "cool lips," whatever they are, and lightning and elephantine play on words.[10] The audience's feeling will be "Oh, go on and die." If Ted had written that scene you'd laugh it out of the window.

You are simply tired of the best scenes because you've read them too much and, having dropped the pilot, you're having the aforesaid pleasure of a child with a box of chalk. You are *or have been* a good writer, but this is a job you will be ashamed of before it's over. The little fluttering life of what's left of my lines and situations won't save the picture.

Example number 3000 is taking out the piano scene between Pat and Köster and substituting garage hammering. Pat the girl who hangs around the garage! And the re-casting of lines—I feel *somewhat outraged.*[11]

Lenz and Bobby's * scene on page 62 [12] isn't even in the same category with my scene. It's dull and solemn, and Köster on page 44 [13] is as uninteresting a plodder as I've avoided in a long life.

What does scene 116 mean? [14] I can just hear the boys relaxing from tension and giving a cheer.

And Pat on page 72—"books and music—she's going to teach him." [15] My God, Joe, you must see what you've done. This isn't Pat—it's a graduate of Pomona College or one of more bespectacled ladies in Mrs. Farrow's department. Books and music! Think, man! Pat is a lady—a cultured European—a charming woman. And Bobby playing soldier. And Pat's really *re*-fined talk about the flower

---

* Bobby's name was changed to Erich in the later revises.—Ed.

garden. They do everything but play ring-around-a-rosie on their Staten Island honeymoon. Recognizable characters they simply are not, and cutting the worst lines here and there isn't going to restore what you've destroyed. It's all so inconsistent. I thought we'd decided long ago what we wanted Pat to be!

On page 74 we meet Mr. Sheriff [16] again, and they say just the cutest merriest things and keep each other in gales of girlish laughter.

On page 93 God begins to come into the script with a vengeance, *but to say in detail what I think of these lines would take a book.* [17] The last pages that everyone liked begin to creak from 116 on, and when I finished there were tears in my eyes, but not for Pat—for Margaret Sullavan.

My only hope is that you will *have a moment of clear thinking. That you'll ask some intelligent* and *disinterested* person to look at the two scripts. Some honest thinking would be much more valuable to the enterprise right now than an effort to convince people you've improved it. I am utterly miserable at seeing months of work and thought negated in one hasty week. I hope you're big enough to take this letter as it's meant—a desperate plea to restore the dialogue to its former quality—to put back the flower cart, the piano-moving, the balcony, the manicure girl—all those touches that were both natural and new. Oh, Joe, can't producers ever be wrong? I'm a good writer—honest. I thought you were going to play fair. Joan Crawford might as well play the part now, for the thing is as groggy with sentimentality as *The Bride Wore Red,* but the true emotion is gone. [18]

Mankiewicz has stated that he never received this letter, which survives in a carbon copy in Fitzgerald's papers. Since there is no closing on the letter, it is possible that Fitzgerald did not send it.*

As the screenplay evolved, its political content became more pointedly anti-Nazi, although the Nazis were not identified. A private screening was arranged for the German consul in Los Angeles, who naturally objected to the anti-Nazi

---

* Mankiewicz's files were destroyed by fire in 1951; none of his material for *Three Comrades* survives.

material in *Three Comrades*. It was suggested to Mankiewicz by Joseph Breen, the industry censor, that the movie could be altered to show that it was about the communists—not the Nazis. Mankiewicz refused to accommodate the Germans and threatened to resign from M.G.M. He remembers, "The next day I went into the commissary, and Scott was there. He ran up, threw his arms around me, and kissed me." [19]

Before *Three Comrades* was released, it was previewed for the exhibitors, who complained about the ending. The 1 February 1938 screenplay and the released print both end with Koster and Erich visiting the graves of Pat and Lenz before leaving Germany for South America. As they walk away from the cemetery, they are joined by the shadowy figures of Pat and Lenz. Fitzgerald wrote to M.G.M. executive producers Eddie Mannix and Sam Katz a letter which he preserved with the notation "Unsent—needless to say":

Dear Sirs:

I have long finished my part in the making of Three Comrades but Mank—— has told me what the exhibitors are saying about the ending and I can't resist a last word. If they had pronounced on Captain's Courageous at this stage, I feel they would have had Manuel the Protugese live and go out west with the little boy and Captain's Courageous could have stood that much better than Three Comrades can stand an essential change in its story. In writing over a hundred and fifty stories for George Lorimer, the great editor of the Saturday Evening Post I found he made a sharp distinction between a sordid tragedy and a heroic tragedy—hating the former but accepting the latter as an essential and interesting part of life.

I think in Three Comrades we run the danger of having the wrong head go on the right body—a thing that confuses and depresses everyone except the ten year olds who are so confused anyhow that I can't believe they make or break a picture. To every reviewer or teacher in America, the idea of the comrades going back into the fight in the spirit of "My Head is Bloody but unbowed" is infinitely stronger and more cheerful than that they should be quitting—all the fine talk, the death of their friends and countrymen in vain. All right, they were suckers, but they were always that in one sense and if it was despicable what was the use of telling their story?

The public will feel this—they feel what they can't express—otherwise we'd change our conception of Chinese palaces and French scientists to fit the conception of hill billies who've never seen palaces or scientists. The public will be vaguely confused by the confusion in our mind—they'll know that the beginning and end don't fit together and when one is confused one rebels by kicking the thing altogether out of mind. Certainly this step of putting in the "new life" thought will not please or fool anyone—it simply loses us the press and takes out of the picture the real rhythm of the ending which is:

The march of four people, living and dead, heroic and inconquerable, side by side back into the fight.[20]

It is not clear what the exhibitors wanted, but it is a safe guess that they objected to Pat's death. Fitzgerald's letter to Mannix and Katz indicates that he wanted to show Koster and Erich returning to the fight against the Nazis. He was overruled.

The movie was released in June 1938, and Fitzgerald's prediction about its failure was wrong. It was a marked success, making the best-10 lists for the year. Margaret Sullavan received an Academy Award nomination, as well as the New York Critics Award and the British National Award.

Three Comrades was the only screen credit Fitzgerald received. He worked out his M.G.M. contract on *Infidelity, The Women, Marie Antoinette,* and *Madame Curie;* but none of his screenplays was produced. After M.G.M. dropped his option in 1939, Fitzgerald freelanced at other studios before starting *The Last Tycoon*—which, in its unfinished state, is the best Hollywood novel ever written.[21] In 1977 Hollywood turned *The Last Tycoon* into the worst movie ever made.

F. Scott Fitzgerald died in Hollywood on 21 December 1940. His last stand in Hollywood occupied forty-two months—eighteen on the M.G.M. payroll. The question of how good a screenwriter Fitzgerald really was remains open, for critics have disagreed. After *Three Comrades* Fitzgerald found no satisfaction in movie work and relinquished his hopes for a new career. He hated the drudgery of movie writing and resented the authority exercised over him by lesser talents. Nonetheless, Hollywood was good for—if not good to—Fitzgerald. He was not a broken hack working on cheap movies. His Pat Hobby stories are not a self-portrait. Hollywood money enabled Fitzgerald to reconstruct his life. At the end he was writing as well as ever. But he was writing a novel.

NOTES

1. Fitzgerald went to Hollywood in 1927 to write an original flapper story, "Lipstick," for Constance Talmadge at United Artists.

2. In 1931 Fitzgerald wrote a screenplay for *Red-Headed Woman* at M.G.M., which was not used. He was hired by Irving Thalberg, who became the model for Monroe Stahr in *The Last Tycoon*.

3. *The Letters of F. Scott Fitzgerald*, ed. Andrew Turnbull (New York: Scribners, 1963), pp. 16–17. ALS, Fitzgerald Papers, Princeton University Library.

4. Carbon copy, Fitzgerald Papers, Princeton University Library.

5. Fitzgerald Papers, Princeton University Library. The wire was forwarded from Asheville to Charleston, S.C. where Fitzgerald had taken Zelda on a furlough from the hospital. IMPOSSIBLE refers to a Goldwynism: "I can tell you in two words—im possible." The wire has been previously published in Aaron Latham, *Crazy Sundays* (New York: Viking, 1971), p. 130.

6. *Letters*, pp. 558–60. Carbon copy, Fitzgerald Papers, Princeton University Library.

7. Fitzgerald Papers, Princeton University Library.

8. Fitzgerald Papers, Princeton University Library.

9. Jacques Bontemps and Richard Overstreet, "Measure for Measure: Interviews with Joseph Mankiewicz," *Cahiers du Cinema in English*, 18 (February 1967), 31.

10. The scene in the sanitarium between Erich and Pat before her operation. Sequence 278 (21 January 1938). See Appendix A.

11. The scene in which Koster urges Pat to marry Erich. Sequence 92 (21 January 1938). See Appendix A.

12. The scene in which Lenz urges Erich to marry Pat. Sequence 91 (21 January 1938). See Appendix A.

13. Dialogue between Lenz and Erich after his first date with Pat. Sequence 66 (21 January 1938). See Appendix A.

14. After the wedding ceremony: "The doors to the kitchen open, and the waiters enter carrying trays of food. This entrance is the signal for a general release of tension. There is general cheering and laughter, and a fine spirited choir from the phonograph. Pat goes back into Erich's arms, and Lenz goes to the bar—"

15. Dialogue between Pat and Erich on their honeymoon. Sequence 121 (21 January 1938). See Appendix A.

16. A reference to the English writer, R. C. Sheriff. Dialogue between Pat and Erich on their honeymoon. Sequence 122 (21 January 1938). See Appendix A.

17. Dialogue between Erich and Pat after their return to Berlin. Sequence 182 (21 January 1938). Erich: It seems to me we're lucky. When I think of life as it was before—I thank God for you.

18. *Letters*, pp. 563–64. Carbon copy, Fitzgerald Papers, Princeton University Library.

19. Aaron Latham, *Crazy Sundays* (New York: Viking Press, 1971), p. 146. Latham does not cite a source for this statement.

20. *Letters*, pp. 565–66. Carbon copy, Fitzgerald Papers, Princeton University Library.

21. See Bruccoli, *"The Last of the Novelists": F. Scott Fitzgerald and The Last Tycoon* (Carbondale: Southern Illinois University Press, 1977).

Appendix A

Revisions

Note: These are the revisions Fitzgerald protested in his 20 January 1938 letter to Mankiewicz.

Sequence 278 (21 January 1938)

Pat

Is that the road home?

Erich

Yes. In May you'll be starting home along that road—

Pat (unbelievingly)

In May—my God, in May.
          (a pause, then she turns to him)
But we're not saying what we should be saying this first time together.
          (he looks at her puzzled)
All these months I'd figured out what you would say and I would say—word for word. Do you want to hear?
          (he nods, smiling)
We'd be sitting here on the foot of this bed like this, hand in hand, and you'd ask, what time is it and I'd say that doesn't matter now. We love each other beyond time and place now. And you'd say, that's right. God's in this room with us, lightning's in this room and the sea and the sky and the

mountains are in this room with us. And you'd kiss me on the forehead and I'd say, how cool your lips are, don't move away—

> (he kisses her on the forehead)

And you'd say, ought I to be in this room now? Aren't we breaking the rules? And I'd say must I start now—not breaking them—

> (he looks into her eyes, unsmiling)

because I can't let you go and then you'd say hello, Pat, and I'd say, Erich, hello, and suddenly it would all be so real it would stab my heart and—

Erich

But—darling—

> They embrace each other fiercely. The CAMERA TRUCKS over their heads to the window, until the window frames disappear and only the snow-covered mountains stand before us.

In the 21 December 1937 version (sequence 310) the scene reads:

Pat

Is that the road home?

Erich

Yes.

Pat

How far is it?

Erich

About five hundred miles. In May you'll be starting back along that road.

Pat (unbelievingly)

In May—my God, in May.

Sequence 92 (21 January 1938)

> INT. REPAIR SHOP — NIGHT
>
> Pat is sitting on the running board of the taxi, which Koster is repairing. He is hammering out a fender which was badly bashed. Most of the damage has already been repaired. Koster punctuates his speech with hammer blows. The scene is illuminated by "Baby's" headlights.

Koster (tapping lightly)

Well, what's wrong about Erich?

Pat (lazily lying down on the running board)

Nothing's wrong about Erich. Erich's—
                    (she restrains herself from saying more)
all right. What's that you're playing with the hammer? Schubert?

Koster (tapping fancily)

Mendelssohn—or do I offend your political beliefs?
                    (she laughs)
Let me give you Erich in a nutshell.

Pat

He'd look cute in a nutshell, but if you don't mind—

Koster (breaking in)

Ability to make a living, better than average. Honesty—ten

percent off for South America, but that leaves ninety.
Spirit—all there is—

Pat

Otto, stick to your music. You're telling me things I know.

Koster

Then why don't you marry him?

Pat (after a moment—evasively)

He hasn't asked me.

Koster

He's scared. Why don't you ask him?
> He has stopped hammering and stands looking at
> her. She smiles up at him.

Pat

That was lovely music, Otto. Let's have some Beethoven—or
no, I imagine Wagner's easier with a hammer
> Koster hesitates a moment, then he goes back to
> his hammering, a little harder now.

Koster

You love each other—you've everything to live for. What
if Germany *has* gone mad? You're sane.
> (he hammers once viciously)
There's hope in both of you, and shelter for the future.

Pat

—and candy stars in a muslin sky.
> (she sits up and looks at Otto)
Let's talk about something else, Otto.

Koster

It's each other you want, Pat—never mind about anything else. Half the troubles in the world come from worrying about what might happen.

Pat (suddenly emotional)

But it wouldn't work! It wouldn't be fair to him!

Koster (quickly)

Why not?

Pat (covering)

I don't know. I—I guess I was born into irresponsibility. Then the war taught me not to take even that too seriously—I guess, Otto, nothing can ever be very important to me.

> She sounds convincing enough. Koster quits working and goes over to her.

Koster

You mustn't ever lie to *me*, Pat.

Pat

No. I musn't.
              (getting up)
So don't ask me any more questions.

Koster (levelly)

I'll *tell* you what's the matter with you. You're scare of suffering—scared of having any joy in your life, because it will make it all the harder when you lose it. You're afraid!

Pat

That's it, let's leave it at that!
> She is desperately unhappy. Koster looks at her
> compassionately, but only because she is not look-
> ing at him.

Koster

Now you're not being fair, Pat. You've got to think of Erich,
now. You're being a coward, you're being selfish—
> Pat leans against the car. She doesn't look at him.

Pat (quietly)

That's—not true.

Koster

Then—what is true, Pat?

Pat (after a moment, still without looking at him)

I told you once I'd been very ill. I'm just patched up now.
It will come back.
> Koster looks at her as if his heart would break.

Koster

Your lungs?
> She nods. He puts an arm around her, tenderly.
> She turns to him, suddenly.

Pat

Otto, don't let me marry him!

Koster

You've got to, Pat—

Pat

But he'll want a happiness that lasts! A home, children—a future that doesn't exist from day to day!

Koster

He wants you—

Pat

But I'm no good, he has a right to more than me!

Koster

Then live, Pat! Take the gamble! Stake your life against a love like yours and Erich's every time! You can only win—if it's an hour, Pat, you can only win!

Pat (after a moment)

I'd have to tell him—

Koster

No. That's part of it. Don't make him afraid; just make him happy. Play to the limit—aim at the stars—
> Slowly she walks to the window. She looks up at the sky. Koster follows her with his eyes.

Pat

Do you suppose they'd mind if we aimed at them?
> (she turns to Koster)

I was told once that the very nearest star is forty million miles away—

In the 21 December 1937 version (sequences 110-113) the scene reads:

INT. PAT'S LIVING ROOM

Pat and Koster seated on opposite sides of tea wagon in front of fire. Koster leans over toward her and speaks with patient concern.

Koster

Pat—why don't you marry Erich?
                    (Pat starts)
You love him, don't you?
            There is the sound of several chords being struck on the piano. The CAMERA PULLS BACK to show on the other side of the room the door open and a blond faded eager little man standing by the grand piano. Behind him in the doorway two moving men are entering.

Blond Man

Oh, I beg your pardon—I can't keep my hands off it. I've brought my movers. They told me to come right in and get it.

Pat

That's all right.

CLOSE SHOT—PAT AND KOSTER

Pat (lying)

It's too big for the apartment.
            Koster understands too well but, full of his purpose he stands up and returns to his subject. His speech is several times punctuated by soft piano chords struck by the piano purchaser.

Koster

Think what you two have together—the one thing that is real and worthwhile in Germany today. That's what Erich needs—something real to live for. The world has somehow slipped away from Lenz and me—I don't want it to happen to Erich. If there was ever a time when love is the only thing to cling to—if you're lucky enough to have it—that time is *now!*

(Eight piano chords struck here)

And Erich is a special kind of man, Pat. He doesn't want just a sweetheart—he wants a wife. Not being married to you, he feels uncertain and insecure. He torments himself with the thought that he might lose you. Believe me—I *know* him.

He looks at Pat to see the effect of his speech.

CUT TO:

THE PIANO

— being pushed gently into the hall. The eager little man is walking beside it and now with one hand he reaches over and plays the first bars of "The Moonlight Sonata."

CUT TO:

PAT —

Pat

What have I got to give him, Otto. Oh, it doesn't make sense—perhaps another kind of woman — who can give him a home and children.

Koster (interrupting passionately)

No, Pat. You're the only possible woman for him.

Pat — now on her feet but not looking at Koster.

Pat (emotionally)

Oh, can't we just go on as we are? Because Otto, even if what you say is true it still wouldn't be fair to him.

> Koster reacts sharply to this, sits down, looks at her a moment in silence. Pat drops her gaze sadly, then looks up at him. Koster takes her hand in his.

Koster

Pat — is it your lungs?

Pat

Yes.

Koster

I see.

Pat

I'm merely patched up. I have to live very carefully. It may come back.

Koster (looks at her narrowly)

And it may *not*. Take the gamble, Pat. Stake a love like yours and Erich's against your life every time! Don't you see that whatever happens — neither of you can *lose*?

> (Pat looks up enquiringly — a piano chord
> from the doorway is bright and challenging)

Take your happiness with both hands — and even if it breaks — you will know — that you've had the only thing worth having in this world.

Pat

I'd have to tell him.

Koster

No, no. That's part of the gamble. Don't worry him. Don't spoil his happiness by bringing fear into it. Play it up to the limit — aim at the stars!

Pat (sadly)

The stars — they're so far away.
>The piano, out of the room now echoes with one sad, minor chord like a goodbye, as we —
>>DISSOLVE TO:

Sequence 91 (21 January 1938)

>INT. ALFONS' BAR — NOON

>Lenz and Erich face each other across a table. Erich, in an oil-stained undershirt, is gulping a dish of stew. Lenz, similarly attired, sits over his coffee. He watches Erich swallow his food —

Lenz (thoughtfully)

What is it about love that makes a man swallow his food whole instead of chewing it?

Erich (not looking up)

Huh?

Lenz (indicating the stew)

That all belongs to you. Nobody's going to steal it. I've had my lunch —
>(he steals a piece of meat with his fingers)
What's going to happen with you and Pat?

Erich

Why should anything happen?

Lenz

You're in love. Why don't you get married?

Erich

We're in love. Isn't that enough?

Lenz

No. You're as fed up with drifting as I am. Somewhere there's a battle going on, and I'm not in it — and somewhere there's a home to be made, and love to be had —

Erich

Well?

Lenz

Marry Pat —

Erich (suddenly)

How can I? Don't you think I've wanted to, don't you know it's the only thing I want? What have I got to offer a girl like that? Nothing now, and nothing to look forward to —

Lenz

Marry her, anyway. Then you'll both have that —

Erich

It's not enough to give her —

Lenz

No one will ever have any more.
                    (he gets up, puts a hand on Erich's shoulder)
This is the right time, believe me. And sometimes it comes
— and goes so quickly that you've lost it forever —
            He leaves. Erich looks after him.

In the 21 December 1937 version (sequence 109) the scene reads:

INT. ALFONS' BAR — NOON

Erich, in an oilstained undershirt, sprawls along
a bench in a booth, his arm black to the elbow
with grease. Poised above him stands Lisa, a good-
looking girl, part time manicurist and a full time
tramp. A manicure case rests beside her as she
looks at Erich with admiration.

Lenz sits alone over his coffee at the next table.
Bobby is in a relaxed mood.

Lisa (looking at his arms)

Of course, you can't eat your lunch like that. I think it's
a good thing I happened to come in.
                    (a waiter sets a bowl of steaming water on
                    the table. She takes off her coat and during
                    the following dialogue sets to work cleaning
                    Erich's arms)
Thanks . . . I wouldn't know those was the same hands that
play the piano so beautiful for us.
                    (eyes his hands determinedly)
This is going to be some job.

Lenz (who is also a little greasy)

Nobody ever did that for me.

Lisa

Erich's different. He's really just a boy, aren't you, dear?

Erich (Shrinking from her ministrations)

Oh, cut it out! I want to drink a beer and get back to work.

Lisa

Now you just sit quiet.
> (She opens her case and after fumbling with lingerie, produces a battered manicure set. Lenz watches cynically as she sets to work)

Lenz

Erich is unhappy, Lisa. You can't reach him thru his fingernails.

Lisa (quickly ruining three towels on Erich)

There — at least I can see your arms. Why is he unhappy?

Lenz

He has Hamlet's trouble — to be or not to be?

Erich (to Lenz)

Cut it out — will you!

Lisa

Now you sit quiet while I get more water.
> She goes o.s.

Lenz

Why not face it? You're as fed up with drifting along as I am. Somewhere there's a battle going on and I'm not in

on it, and somewhere there's a home to be made and love
to be had.

Erich

Is that a reference to me?

Lenz

Don't get jumpy. You know it's true — how long have you
known Pat?

Erich

About two months.

Lenz

They why don't you marry her?

Erich (astounded)

Me marry Pat? What have I got to offer a girl like that?
Living from hand to mouth — no prospects. She'd never marry
me in a thousand years.
            Lisa comes back into scene.

Lisa

Who wouldn't marry you? I don't blame them. It wouldn't
be fair to all the other girls.

Lenz

Come on, Lisa. You know Erich never made love to you.

Lisa (wistfully)

Well, he always has that look — as if he was just going to.
            Lenz gets up and comes over to Erich.

Lenz (hand on Erich's shoulder)

I know the obstacles — I know everything you're thinking —

Lisa

Now give me your hand.
                    (resentfully to Lenz)
How do *you* know what Erich's thinking?

Lenz (paying no attention)

— but sometimes the right time comes — and then goes so quickly that you've lost it forever.

Sequence 66 (21 January 1938)

INT. REPAIR SHOP

as Lenz enters. Erich sits disconsolately at the desk. He looks up without much interest.

Lenz (spilling coins on desk)

Three marks' profit over and above the water pump, which died, and the cost of the license and cap.
                    (as he takes off the cap)
Drunks tip the best, and old ladies don't tip at all. There's a moral there, somewhere. Here's the cap.

Erich doesn't answer, but continues looking gloomily off into space.

Lenz

What's the matter with you?

Erich (slowly)

I'm in a mess. I've completely ruined myself with Pat. That's what I've done.

> (Lenz looks at Erich amused, while he goes
> through his pockets for a cigarette)

She's probably used to millionaires and counts and how they
behave. I acted like a drunken sot.

Lenz (laughs)

What do you think millionaires act like — millionaires? It's
too bad, though. I guess I should have stayed at Alfons' to
take care of you.

> (with a touch of seriousness)

That might have been better — for all of us.

> Erich looks up sharply. It is his turn now to be
> alarmed.

Erich

What happened at your meeting — another riot?

Lenz (shakes his head)

But some of the busy little book-burners followed me home.

Erich

Oh —

> (back to his own troubles)

Gottfried, you know about such things — South America,
and all that. What does a man do — how does he apologize?

Lenz

He doesn't. If you're going to apologize for everything that
goes wrong in this world, who'll start it?

Erich

But I behaved like an idiot!

Lenz

Send flowers. They cover everything. Even graves.
> (he claps the taxi cap on Erich's head)

Come on, go to work —
> (as they move to the door)

Be careful of that radiator — don't take anybody up hills —
> Together they exit from office.

Sequence 121 (21 January 1938)

Erich

There, you see. I was afraid of that. You're bored —

Pat

No, I'm not —

Erich

You will be, soon. What on earth are we going to talk about for the rest of our lives?

Pat (turns back, smiling now)

You —

Erich

Twelve minutes, by the clock —

Pat

Me, then —

Erich

We couldn't talk. We'd have to sing —

Pat

Darling. Books and music. They're always safe —

Erich

I don't know anything about books, and I don't know anything about music —

Pat

I'll teach you. It's time you went to school —

Sequence 122 (21 January 1938)

Pat

Listen. A cuckoo bird —

Erich

That makes three of us —

Pat

I've been counting. For every time he calls — you have that number of years to live —

Erich

There's a better one than that. When a cuckoo calls, rattle your money and it multiplies —

Pat

Eighteen, nineteen, twenty —

Erich

Only I haven't got any money to rattle. That cuckoo's making a fool of himself —

Pat

Twenty three, twenty four, twenty five —

Erich

Imagine. Our silver wedding. Our beautiful daughter has married the only millionaire left in the world, and gone to the North Pole to live —

Pat

Twenty eight, twenty nine —

Erich

Our handsome son and heir has left college, and refused to go to war. Thrown into jail for the rest of his life —

Pat

Thirty one, thirty two —

Erich

We are now all alone again — a sweet, silver-haired old couple —
                    (he gets up)
I'm hungry. You can come back tomorrow, and count cuckoos all day —

Appendix B
Fitzgerald's Movie Work

Glimpses of the Moon. Famous players, 1923. Titles.

Grit. Film Guild, 1924.

"Lipstick." United Artists, 1927. Unproduced.

Red-Headed Woman. M.G.M., 1931. Screenplay not used.

A Yank at Oxford. M.G.M., 1937. Dialogue polish.

Three Comrades. M.G.M., 1937–38. Screen credit as co-author of screenplay.

"Infidelity." M.G.M., 1938. Unproduced.

Marie Antoinette. M.G.M., 1938. Screenplay not used.

The Women. M.G.M., 1938. Screenplay not used.

Madame Curie. M.G.M., 1938. Screenplay not used.

Gone With the Wind. Selznick, 1939. Two weeks?—dialogue polish.

Winter Carnival. United Artists, 1939. Dismissed.

"Air Raid." Paramount, 1939. Unproduced.

"Open that Door." Universal, 1939. One week.

Everything Happens at Night. 20th Century-Fox, 1939. One day.

Raffles. Goldwyn, 1939. One week.

"Cosmopolitan." ("Babylon Revisited"). Columbia, 1940. Unproduced.

"Brooklyn Bridge." 20th Century-Fox, 1940. Fitzgerald's assignment unknown.

Life Begins at Eight-Thirty (The Light of Heart). 20th Century-Fox, 1940. Screenplay not used.